TRADING

FOR

I0446516

BEGINNERS

ARSENE JUNIOR JOSEPH

Table of Contents

Foreword

Trading can be a thrilling and rewarding journey, but for beginners, it can also be a daunting and complex world to navigate. This book, "Trading for Beginners," serves as a guiding light for those embarking on this exciting adventure in the financial markets.

In the rapidly evolving landscape of finance, the art of trading has never been more accessible, thanks to technological advancements and the democratization of information. Yet, with this accessibility comes a greater need for knowledge and understanding, for as the saying goes, "With great power comes great responsibility."

The pages that follow are a treasure trove of insights, strategies, and practical advice carefully crafted to help aspiring traders grasp the fundamentals of trading. Whether you're intrigued by stocks, forex, commodities, or cryptocurrencies, this book offers a comprehensive roadmap to start your trading journey.

From the very beginning, you'll be introduced to the financial markets, uncovering their history, importance, and the various assets they encompass. You'll gain a firm grasp of risk management, technical and fundamental analysis, and how to set up your trading environment with the right broker, platform, and tools.

But this book goes beyond theory. It provides you with an array of real life examples, case studies, and anecdotes from successful traders who've walked the path before you. These stories illustrate the challenges and triumphs of the trading world, offering valuable lessons and inspiration.

"Trading for Beginners" is divided into three parts: Building a Foundation, Trading Strategies, and Trading Psychology and Practice. Each section delves into the core elements of trading, equipping you with the knowledge to make informed decisions in the financial markets.

As you navigate these pages, you'll discover a wealth of trading strategies, both technical and fundamental, suitable for various trading styles. These strategies are not presented in isolation; they are complemented by practical guidance on risk management, trading plans, and the critical aspects of trading psychology. After all, successful trading is not only about analyzing charts and data; it's also about managing your emotions and maintaining discipline.

In closing, let this book be your trusted companion as you embark on your trading journey. Remember that trading is a continuous learning process, and the experiences and lessons within these pages are meant to serve as your foundation. The path may be challenging at times, but with dedication, patience, and a solid understanding of the principles outlined here, you can navigate the financial markets with confidence.

Whether your goal is financial independence, wealth accumulation, or simply a deeper understanding of the world of trading, this book is your first step towards achieving those aspirations. So, embrace the knowledge within, practice diligently, and may your trading endeavors be both rewarding and fulfilling.

Best wishes on your journey into the world of trading!

Arsene Junior Joseph

ACKNOWLEDGMENTS

First and foremost, I would like to express my deepest gratitude to Jesus Christ, whose boundless love, guidance, and grace have been the foundation of my life and the inspiration behind this book. Without His presence and unwavering support, this journey would not have been possible.

To my beloved wife, Rose Andree Marjorie, your unwavering love, encouragement, and understanding have been my greatest source of strength throughout this endeavor. Your belief in me and this project has been a constant source of motivation.

I want to extend my heartfelt thanks to my dear friend Raguel Figaro for your invaluable insights, encouragement, and prayers. Your wisdom and unwavering support have enriched the pages of this book.

To India Jean Pierre, your friendship and thoughtful discussions have been instrumental in shaping the ideas and concepts presented in these chapters. Your feedback and perspective have been invaluable.

I am also grateful for the technology that made this project possible. whose assistance and collaboration have been instrumental in bringing this book to life.

To all those who have supported and believed in me along this journey, whether mentioned here or not, your presence and contributions have been deeply appreciated. Thank you all.

FOR WHOM IS THIS BOOK?

"This book, "Trading for Beginners," is intended for individuals who are new to the world of trading and want to build a solid foundation of knowledge and skills. It is designed for:

1. **Novice Traders:** If you have little to no prior experience in trading but are eager to learn, this book is an excellent starting point. It provides a step-by-step approach, beginning with the basics, to help you understand the key concepts and practices in trading.

2. **Investors Transitioning to Active Trading:** If you've been an investor but are looking to become an active trader, this book will help you make the transition. It covers various trading strategies and techniques, both technical and fundamental, to assist you in making more informed trading decisions.

3. **Aspiring Financial Market Participants:** Whether you're interested in trading stocks, forex, commodities, cryptocurrencies, or any other financial instrument, this book offers a broad overview of the different markets, allowing you to explore the options available and choose the ones that align with your interests.

4. **Individuals Seeking Financial Literacy:** Even if your primary goal is not to become a trader, understanding the fundamentals of trading and investment can enhance your financial literacy. This knowledge can be valuable for making informed financial decisions and managing your investments more effectively.

5. **Those Wanting to Improve Trading Skills:** If you're already engaged in trading but wish to refine your skills, this book provides a comprehensive review of key concepts, strategies, and best practices that can help you become a more proficient trader.

6. **Anyone Interested in Financial Markets:** If you're simply curious about how financial markets work, this book offers a clear and

accessible introduction. It aims to demystify the world of trading and provide you with the knowledge necessary to navigate it with confidence.

Please note that while this book is designed for beginners, trading involves risks, and there are no guarantees of profit. It is essential to approach trading with caution, discipline, and a commitment to continuous learning. This book serves as a valuable starting point on your trading journey, but your success ultimately depends on your dedication, practice, and ability to adapt to the dynamic nature of the financial markets."

INTRODUCTION

Trading for Beginners is a comprehensive guide designed to equip newcomers to the world of trading with the knowledge and skills necessary to navigate the financial markets successfully. In this book, we will explore the core principles, strategies, and tools that form the foundation of trading. Whether you are interested in stocks, forex, cryptocurrencies, or other assets, this guide will provide you with a solid understanding of the trading fundamentals.

Trading can be a rewarding endeavor, offering opportunities for financial growth and independence. However, it also comes with its share of complexities and risks. That's why it's crucial for beginners to start with a solid grasp of the basics. This book aims to demystify the world of trading, making it accessible and understandable to anyone willing to learn.

Throughout the chapters, we will cover topics such as the history of money, different trading methods, technical and fundamental analysis, risk management, and much more. Each chapter will be filled with detailed explanations, real-world examples, and practical advice to help you build a strong foundation in trading.

Whether you aspire to become a full-time trader or simply want to enhance your financial literacy, Trading for Beginners will serve as your comprehensive roadmap on this exciting journey. By the time you finish reading this book, you will be better equipped to make informed trading decisions and embark on your trading adventure with confidence. So, let's dive into the world of trading and explore the endless possibilities it offers to those willing to learn and adapt.

DEFINITION OF TRADING

Trading refers to the buying and selling of financial instruments or assets in the financial markets with the intention of making a profit. It involves the exchange of ownership or rights to an asset, such as stocks, bonds, currencies, commodities, or cryptocurrencies, between individuals, institutions, or entities.

Trading can take various forms, including:

1. **Stock Trading:** Buying and selling shares or equities in publicly traded companies through stock exchanges.

2. **Forex Trading:** Trading in the foreign exchange market, where participants exchange one currency for another in the hope of profiting from currency price fluctuations.

3. **Commodity Trading:** Buying and selling physical commodities like gold, oil, agricultural products, or futures contracts tied to these commodities.

4. **Cryptocurrency Trading:** Trading digital currencies like Bitcoin, Ethereum, and others on cryptocurrency exchanges.

5. **Options and Futures Trading:** Engaging in derivative markets by buying or selling options and futures contracts based on underlying assets.

6. **Day Trading:** A short-term trading strategy where traders buy and sell assets within the same trading day, aiming to profit from intraday price movements.

7. **Swing Trading:** A trading style that seeks to capitalize on short to medium-term price swings in financial instruments.

8. **Long-term Investing:** Buying assets with the intention of holding them for an extended period, often years, with the goal of capital appreciation or income generation.

9. **Algorithmic Trading:** The use of computer algorithms to execute trading strategies automatically, often at high speeds, in response to predefined criteria or signals.

Trading requires a good understanding of financial markets, analysis techniques (technical and fundamental), risk management, and trading strategies. It is important to note that trading involves risks, and individuals should approach it with caution, conduct thorough research, and often start with a well-thought-out trading plan to manage those risks and increase the likelihood of achieving their financial goals.

Chapter 1

The History of Money

Money, as we know it today, is the lifeblood of modern economies, facilitating trade, enabling transactions, and serving as a store of value. But the concept of money, and its various forms throughout history, has evolved significantly. In this chapter, we'll embark on a journey through time, exploring the fascinating history of money, from its humble beginnings to the sophisticated financial systems we have today.

The Origins of Money

The history of money can be traced back thousands of years, to a time when early civilizations engaged in barter trade. In these primitive societies, people exchanged goods and services directly, relying on a system of barter where one item was swapped for another. However, barter had inherent limitations. It required a double coincidence of wants, meaning both parties had to want what the other had to offer. This limitation made trade cumbersome and inefficient, prompting the need for a more efficient medium of exchange.

The Emergence of Commodity Money

As societies grew more complex, so did their economic needs. Around 3,000 BC, societies began using commodity money, which consisted of valuable items with intrinsic worth. These items, such as shells, salt, cattle, and grain, became widely accepted as a medium of exchange because they were valuable in and of themselves and could be easily traded. For instance, cowrie shells were used as money in many parts of the world, including Africa, Asia, and the Pacific Islands.

The Birth of Metal Coinage

The transition from commodity money to metal coinage was a significant leap in the evolution of money. The first metal coins, made from metals like copper, silver, and gold, appeared around 600 BC in the ancient kingdoms of Lydia and China. These coins were standardized in terms of weight and purity, making them a trusted medium of exchange. The value of metal coins was based on their weight and metal content, which led to the development of standardized units and denominations.

One remarkable example of early metal coinage is the famous Greek drachma, which featured the image of Athena on one side and an owl on the other. These coins were widely recognized and accepted, not only in Greece but also in neighboring regions, facilitating trade across vast distances.

Paper Money and the Birth of Banking

While metal coins were highly valuable and portable, they were also susceptible to wear and tear. To address this issue, various cultures began using paper money. China, during the Tang Dynasty (7th century AD), is credited with the invention of paper currency. These early banknotes represented a promise to pay the bearer a certain amount of precious metal upon demand. They were more convenient for large transactions and reduced the need to carry heavy metal coins.

In Europe, the Medici family of Florence, Italy, played a pivotal role in the development of modern banking and paper money. In the 15th century, the Medici banks issued promissory notes, which served as a form of paper money and laid the foundation for the modern banking system.

The Gold Standard and Fiat Money

The 19th century witnessed the widespread adoption of the gold standard, where the value of a country's currency was directly linked to a specific quantity of gold. This system provided stability and reassurance to financial markets and international trade. The British pound and the U.S. dollar were among the world's dominant currencies under the gold standard.

However, the gold standard had limitations, including a fixed money supply tied to gold reserves, which could hinder economic growth during times of increased demand for money. In the 20th century, most countries gradually abandoned the gold standard and adopted fiat money, where the value of currency is not backed by a physical commodity but relies on the trust and confidence of the issuing government.

Digital and Cryptocurrency Revolution

The digital age brought about a new era in the history of money. With the advent of computers and the internet, digital currencies became prevalent. Today, the majority of money exists in digital form, stored electronically in banks and financial institutions. Electronic payment systems, such as credit cards and mobile wallets, have become the norm for everyday transactions.

In 2009, the emergence of Bitcoin, the first cryptocurrency, introduced a groundbreaking concept: decentralized digital currency. Bitcoin operates on a blockchain, a distributed ledger technology, and is not controlled by any central authority or government. Its success has inspired the creation of thousands of other cryptocurrencies, each with its unique features and use cases.

The Future of Money

As we stand on the cusp of a new era in the history of money, it's essential to recognize that the concept of money is continually evolving. Emerging technologies like blockchain, central bank digital currencies (CBDCs), and innovations in payment systems are shaping the future of finance. The way we store, transfer, and transact value is undergoing a profound transformation, promising greater efficiency, security, and accessibility in the world of finance.

In conclusion, the history of money is a testament to human ingenuity and adaptability. From primitive barter systems to the sophisticated digital currencies of today, money has continuously evolved to meet the changing needs of society. As we move forward, it is essential to understand this rich history to appreciate the dynamic nature of money and its pivotal role in the global economy.

Chapter 2

Barter and Gold - The Foundations of Money

In the annals of human history, the concept of money did not emerge fully formed. Instead, it evolved gradually from primitive systems of trade and exchange. Chapter 1 delves into two essential elements that laid the foundation for money as we know it today: barter and the allure of gold.

The Barter Dilemma

Imagine a time long ago when human societies were small, and wants were relatively simple. In these early communities, people relied on a system of barter to meet their needs. Barter involved the direct exchange of goods and services, and in its most basic form, it might have looked something like this: a farmer traded a bushel of wheat for a hunter's freshly caught game. However, this seemingly straightforward exchange system faced significant challenges.

The Double Coincidence of Wants

One of the primary obstacles of barter was the requirement for a double coincidence of wants. In other words, for a barter trade to occur, both parties had to want what the other had to offer. If the farmer desired a warm fur coat instead of the hunter's game, no trade could take place, leaving both parties unsatisfied. This inherent limitation of barter made economic transactions cumbersome and unpredictable.

To illustrate this challenge further, consider a more contemporary example. Imagine you have a collection of antique books, and you're interested in acquiring a new laptop. You find someone willing to trade their laptop for your books, but the laptop owner actually wants a bicycle. In such a scenario, the barter process becomes an intricate puzzle of finding someone with precisely what you desire who also wants what you possess, highlighting the impracticality of the barter system.

Commodity Money: The Birth of Convenience

The limitations of barter spurred the evolution of a more convenient medium of exchange: commodity money. Commodity money consisted of items that held intrinsic value, were durable, and could serve as a reliable medium for trade. Among the earliest forms of commodity money were livestock, grains, and even rare seashells, which were used as currency in various ancient societies.

One of the most famous examples of commodity money is gold. Gold's unique properties, such as its scarcity, durability, divisibility, and malleability, made it an ideal choice for use as money. Its intrinsic value, stemming from its beauty and rarity, made it universally desirable, overcoming the double coincidence of wants that plagued barter systems.

The Allure of Gold

The use of gold as a medium of exchange and store of value can be traced back thousands of years. Ancient civilizations, from the Egyptians and Greeks to the Romans and Chinese, recognized gold's worth and employed it as a form of money. These civilizations minted gold coins, each stamped with intricate designs and symbols denoting their authenticity and weight.

One notable example is the ancient Greek drachma, which featured a depiction of the goddess Athena on one side and an owl, a symbol of wisdom, on the other. The drachma was widely accepted in trade and played a pivotal role in the economic prosperity of the Greek city-states.

Gold's Role in Shaping Monetary Systems

As civilizations expanded and economies grew more complex, gold played a central role in shaping monetary systems. The gold standard, a monetary system where the value of a country's currency was directly tied to a specific quantity of gold, became prevalent in the 19th and early 20th centuries. Nations such as Britain and the United States adopted the gold standard, providing stability and confidence in their currencies.

13

Under the gold standard, paper money was backed by physical gold reserves held by central banks. Individuals could exchange their paper currency for actual gold, reinforcing trust in the monetary system. For example, one could exchange a $20 U.S. bill for a one-ounce gold coin, as specified by the gold standard.

Conclusion: The Legacy of Barter and Gold

The history of money is a testament to humanity's ingenuity and adaptability. Barter, with its challenges, paved the way for the development of more efficient mediums of exchange, including commodity money like gold. Gold's unique properties and universal desirability made it a cornerstone of monetary systems for centuries.

Today, while we no longer rely on barter and the gold standard has largely been abandoned, the legacy of these foundational concepts still resonates in our modern financial systems. Understanding the evolution from barter to commodity money helps us appreciate the complex history that has led to the diverse forms of currency and exchange methods we use in our contemporary world.

Chapter 3

Paper Money - The Evolution of Trust

The transition from commodity money, such as gold and silver, to paper money marked a pivotal moment in the history of currency. Paper money, also known as banknotes or bills, revolutionized the way people conducted trade and commerce. In this chapter, we will explore the origins, development, and significance of paper money, and how it transformed economies worldwide.

The Birth of Paper Money

The concept of paper money originated in ancient China during the Tang Dynasty (7th century AD). The Chinese government initially issued these early banknotes as a means to reduce the need for carrying heavy metal coins over long distances. These early banknotes were a practical solution, representing a promise to pay the bearer a specified amount of precious metal, usually gold or silver, upon demand. They were known as "jiaozi" and were widely accepted in both domestic and international trade. One of the earliest known examples of paper money was the "jiaozi" issued by the Chinese government during the Song Dynasty (11th century AD). These banknotes played a vital role in facilitating trade along the Silk Road, where merchants and traders relied on them for secure and convenient transactions.

Europe's Encounter with Paper Money

Although paper money originated in China, its adoption in Europe took several centuries. During the Middle Ages, European economies primarily relied on a mixture of gold and silver coins, along with local currencies issued by various authorities, such as municipalities and banks. It was in the 17th century that European banks began issuing banknotes, with the Bank of England leading the way. The Bank of England's issuance of banknotes, backed by its holdings of gold and silver, laid the foundation for modern paper money systems. These banknotes gained trust and acceptance due to the credibility of the issuing institution and the knowledge that they could be redeemed for precious metals upon request.

15

The Era of Central Banking

The 19th century witnessed the rise of central banks in Europe and North America. These central banks were granted the exclusive right to issue currency, making their banknotes the dominant form of money in their respective countries. The widespread adoption of central banking solidified the role of paper money in the global economy. For example, the United States established the Federal Reserve System in 1913, giving it the authority to issue the U.S. dollar. U.S. dollars became the primary medium of exchange, and the backing of these banknotes transitioned from a strict gold standard to a system of fiat money, where the value of the currency relies on the trust and confidence of the government.

Modern Paper Money: Fiat Currency

In the 20th century, most countries moved away from the gold standard and embraced fiat currency. Fiat money is not backed by a physical commodity like gold or silver but is instead declared legal tender by the government. Its value is derived from the trust and faith that individuals and institutions place in the government's ability to manage the currency responsibly. One example of a fiat currency is the Euro (EUR), used by the member countries of the Eurozone. The Euro has banknotes and coins issued by the European Central Bank (ECB) and national central banks. These banknotes are widely accepted and trusted as a means of payment across multiple countries, despite the absence of a physical backing.

In the modern era, paper money remains an essential part of our daily lives, coexisting with digital forms of payment like credit cards and mobile wallets. Physical banknotes and coins continue to circulate, serving as a tangible representation of a nation's wealth and economy. While the role of paper money has evolved, its significance in facilitating economic transactions, preserving financial stability, and providing a universally accepted medium of exchange remains unquestionable. Even in an increasingly digital world, the legacy of paper money endures as a testament to the evolution of trust and the complexity of our global financial systems.

Chapter 4

The Gold Standard - A Pillar of Monetary Stability

The Gold Standard represents a remarkable chapter in the history of monetary systems. For much of the 19th and early 20th centuries, it stood as a symbol of financial stability, providing a foundation for international trade and exchange rates. In this chapter, we will delve into the origins, workings, and impact of the Gold Standard, as well as its eventual decline and legacy.

The Origins of the Gold Standard

The concept of the Gold Standard can be traced back to ancient civilizations where gold coins were used as currency. However, the modern Gold Standard emerged in the 19th century when countries formalized the link between their national currencies and physical gold. This system gained prominence due to the recognition of gold's intrinsic value, durability, and universal acceptance.

The Key Features of the Gold Standard

Under the Gold Standard, a nation's currency had a fixed exchange rate with a specific quantity of gold. For example, a country might determine that one ounce of gold is equal to ten units of its currency. This fixed rate provided confidence in the value of the currency, as individuals and nations knew that they could exchange their paper money for its equivalent value in gold.

To illustrate, consider the British pound sterling. During the height of the Gold Standard, one pound could be exchanged for 7.32 grams of pure gold, known as a sovereign. This fixed exchange rate allowed businesses and individuals to engage in international trade with a predictable currency exchange, fostering global economic stability.

Advantages of the Gold Standard

One of the primary advantages of the Gold Standard was its ability to limit inflation. Since the supply of gold is relatively stable and limited, it prevented governments from printing excessive amounts of money, which could lead to devaluation and price instability. The Gold Standard encouraged fiscal discipline and responsible monetary policies.

Moreover, the fixed exchange rates of the Gold Standard facilitated international trade. Traders and investors could engage in cross-border transactions without worrying about unpredictable fluctuations in exchange rates. This stability promoted economic growth and investment.

Examples of the Gold Standard in Action

Several countries adopted variations of the Gold Standard during its heyday. The British Empire, with the pound sterling as its anchor currency, was a notable proponent of the Gold Standard. The United States also adopted the Gold Standard in the 19th century, and the U.S. dollar was linked to a fixed quantity of gold.

The Gold Standard played a critical role in the international monetary system. For instance, the Gold Exchange Standard, established in the late 19th century, allowed countries to hold their foreign exchange reserves in the form of gold. This system facilitated the settlement of international trade balances and helped maintain currency stability.

The Decline and End of the Gold Standard

Despite its advantages, the Gold Standard faced challenges. During times of economic crisis or war, governments found it difficult to maintain the fixed exchange rate. The rigid monetary policy of the Gold Standard could exacerbate economic downturns by limiting the flexibility to adjust the money supply.

The system's downfall became evident during World War I when many countries suspended their adherence to the Gold Standard to finance the war effort. After the war, attempts to restore the Gold Standard were made, but the interwar period was marked by economic instability.

The final blow to the Gold Standard came during the Great Depression and World War II. Countries abandoned it in favor of more flexible exchange rate systems. In 1971, President Richard Nixon announced the suspension of the U.S. dollar's convertibility into gold, effectively ending the international Gold Standard.

The Legacy of the Gold Standard

While the Gold Standard is no longer in use, its legacy endures. It serves as a historical benchmark for the stability and discipline it brought to monetary systems. The principles of sound money and fiscal responsibility that it promoted continue to influence modern economic policies and discussions surrounding currency stability.

In conclusion, the Gold Standard remains a symbol of an era when currencies were firmly anchored to tangible assets. Its rise and fall illustrate the complexity of maintaining fixed exchange rates and the challenges faced by nations in times of economic turmoil. Although the Gold Standard has faded into history, its impact on the world of finance and economics is still felt today.

Chapter 5

The Bretton Woods System
A New Era of Global Monetary Order

The Bretton Woods system represents a watershed moment in the history of international finance and monetary cooperation. Conceived amid the chaos of World War II and formalized in 1944, this chapter explores the origins, structure, and significance of the Bretton Woods system, which aimed to restore order to the post-war global economy.

The Context of Post-War Chaos

World War II left much of the global economy in shambles. Europe and Asia were ravaged by conflict, and countries were grappling with immense debts and economic instability. At this critical juncture, world leaders recognized the need for a new international monetary framework that could facilitate economic recovery, prevent competitive currency devaluations, and foster global stability.

The Bretton Woods Conference

In July 1944, representatives from 44 Allied nations gathered in Bretton Woods, New Hampshire, USA, to establish a new international monetary order. The conference resulted in the creation of two key institutions: the International Monetary Fund (IMF) and the International Bank for Reconstruction and Development (IBRD), later known as the World Bank.

The IMF's primary role was to oversee the international monetary system, facilitate exchange rate stability, and provide financial assistance to member countries facing balance of payments problems. The World Bank was tasked with providing long-term loans to help war-torn countries rebuild their economies and infrastructure.

Fixed Exchange Rates and the US Dollar as the Anchor

At the heart of the Bretton Woods system was a commitment to fixed exchange rates. Member countries agreed to peg their currencies to the U.S. dollar, which, in turn, was tied to gold at a rate of $35 per ounce. This fixed rate provided stability to exchange rates and facilitated international trade and investment.

The U.S. dollar emerged as the world's primary reserve currency, known as the "key currency." This role elevated the United States to a position of economic leadership and responsibility within the global monetary system.

The Role of Gold and Convertibility

While the U.S. dollar was pegged to gold, other currencies were pegged to the dollar. This arrangement allowed member countries to exchange their currencies for U.S. dollars at the fixed rate and, if desired, convert those dollars into gold. This gold convertibility feature provided confidence in the system and prevented excessive currency devaluations.

The system's stability was reinforced by a commitment to maintaining exchange rates within a narrow band (1% fluctuation) around the fixed par value. Member countries agreed to adjust their monetary policies and exchange rates as needed to achieve this goal

Successes and Challenges of Bretton Woods

The Bretton Woods system brought a period of relative economic stability and growth to the post-war world. It facilitated the reconstruction of Europe and Japan, promoted international trade, and discouraged competitive devaluations that had characterized the interwar period.

However, the system faced challenges. As the U.S. ran persistent balance of payments deficits due to the costs of the Korean and Vietnam Wars and the expansion of domestic social programs, its gold reserves came under pressure. Concerns about the United States' ability to maintain the $35 per ounce gold convertibility led to doubts about the sustainability of the system.

The End of Bretton Woods

In 1971, President Richard Nixon announced the suspension of U.S. dollar convertibility into gold, effectively ending the Bretton Woods system. This event, known as the "Nixon Shock," marked the beginning of the era of fiat currencies, where currencies were no longer tied to physical assets like gold.

The demise of the Bretton Woods system was a significant turning point in the history of global finance. It ushered in a new era of floating exchange rates and increased currency volatility, while the IMF continued to play a role in promoting monetary stability and providing financial assistance to member countries in need.

The Legacy of Bretton Woods

The Bretton Woods system left a lasting legacy. Its vision of international cooperation and monetary stability served as a blueprint for subsequent international monetary arrangements. The IMF and World Bank continue to operate today, striving to promote global financial stability and economic development.

In conclusion, the Bretton Woods system represented a bold and innovative attempt to bring order to a post-war world in turmoil. While it ultimately faced challenges that led to its demise, its principles of fixed exchange rates, cooperation among nations, and international financial institutions continue to influence the world of finance and economics to this day.

Chapter 6

The End of the Gold Standard
A Monumental Shift in Monetary History

The Gold Standard, a system that had underpinned the global monetary order for decades, met its demise in the early 1970s. This chapter explores the factors, events, and consequences that led to the end of the Gold Standard, marking a significant turning point in the history of international finance and monetary policy.

The Gold Standard's Post-War Resurgence

Following the end of World War II, the Bretton Woods system was established in 1944, which brought a modified version of the Gold Standard back into play. Under Bretton Woods, currencies were pegged to the U.S. dollar, which was itself tied to gold at a fixed rate of $35 per ounce. This system provided stability and confidence in international trade and finance during the post-war era.

The U.S. Dollar's Role and Responsibility

The Bretton Woods system elevated the U.S. dollar to the status of the world's primary reserve currency. As the linchpin of the system, the U.S. committed to maintaining the dollar's convertibility into gold. This responsibility placed immense pressure on the United States to manage its balance of payments effectively and ensure that its gold reserves remained sufficient to meet international demand.

Challenges and Growing Imbalances

Throughout the 1950s and 1960s, the United States faced growing challenges that strained the Bretton Woods system. The costs of the Korean and Vietnam Wars, along with the expansion of domestic social programs, led to persistent balance of payments deficits. As a result, the U.S. gold reserves dwindled, creating concerns about the sustainability of the system.

Speculative Attacks and Gold Outflows

By the late 1960s, mounting doubts about the U.S. dollar's convertibility into gold led to speculative attacks on the dollar. Foreign governments and central banks began converting their excess dollar holdings into gold, putting immense pressure on U.S. gold reserves. This further eroded confidence in the Bretton Woods system.

In 1971, the situation reached a breaking point. President Richard Nixon announced a series of measures that effectively ended the Gold Standard. He suspended the U.S. dollar's convertibility into gold, closed the gold window, and imposed a temporary suspension on gold sales to foreign official institutions. These actions, known as the "Nixon Shock," marked the official end of the Bretton Woods system and the Gold Standard.

Consequences of the End of the Gold Standard

The decision to abandon the Gold Standard had profound implications for the global monetary system and international finance:

1. **Floating Exchange Rates:** With the end of the Gold Standard, currencies began to float freely, allowing their values to be determined by supply and demand in the foreign exchange markets. This introduced a new era of exchange rate volatility.

2. **Increased Currency Risk:** The absence of fixed exchange rates meant that businesses and investors had to contend with currency risk when engaging in international trade and investment.

3. **Shift in Monetary Policy:** Central banks gained greater control over their domestic monetary policies, as they were no longer constrained by the need to maintain fixed exchange rates.

4. **Transition to Fiat Currencies:** Currencies transitioned from being backed by a physical commodity like gold to fiat currencies, whose value relies on the trust and confidence of the issuing government.

5. **Emergence of the IMF:** The International Monetary Fund (IMF) took on a more prominent role in managing global monetary stability and providing financial assistance to member countries facing balance of payments crises.

The Legacy of the Gold Standard's End

The end of the Gold Standard marked the beginning of a new era in international finance. While it eliminated the rigid constraints of fixed exchange rates, it also introduced increased uncertainty and currency volatility. Today, the legacy of the Gold Standard endures as a historical milestone in the evolution of monetary policy and the global financial system. It serves as a reminder of the complex challenges and trade-offs that policymakers face in maintaining international monetary stability.

Chapter 7

What is Trading?

Trading is the heartbeat of financial markets, a dynamic process that drives the buying and selling of various financial instruments, from stocks and currencies to commodities and cryptocurrencies. In this chapter, we will explore the intricacies of trading, its fundamental principles, and the diverse forms it takes in today's global financial landscape.

The Essence of Trading

At its core, trading is the act of buying and selling financial assets with the aim of making a profit. It is a fundamental economic activity that facilitates the allocation of resources and capital within an economy. Trading serves several key purposes, including price discovery, liquidity provision, and risk management.

The Players in Trading

Trading involves a multitude of participants, each with distinct roles and objectives:

1. **Traders:** These individuals or institutions engage in the actual buying and selling of assets. Traders can be individuals, proprietary trading firms, hedge funds, or professional investors.

2. **Market Makers:** Market makers are institutions that facilitate trading by providing liquidity to the market. They continuously quote buy and sell prices for assets, narrowing the bid-ask spread and ensuring smooth trading.

3. **Brokers:** Brokers act as intermediaries between buyers and sellers, executing trades on behalf of clients. They may offer research and trading platforms to assist traders in making informed decisions.

4. **Exchanges:** Exchanges are organized marketplaces where assets are traded. They play a crucial role in ensuring fair and transparent trading by enforcing rules and regulations.

Financial Instruments Traded

Trading encompasses a wide array of financial instruments, each with its unique characteristics:

1. **Stocks:** Trading shares of ownership in publicly listed companies, allowing investors to participate in a company's success and share in its profits through dividends and capital appreciation.

2. **Forex (Foreign Exchange):** Trading currencies from different countries in the world's largest and most liquid financial market. Forex trading involves speculating on currency price movements.

3. **Commodities:** Trading physical goods such as gold, oil, agricultural products, and more. Commodity trading can be done through futures contracts, allowing investors to speculate on price changes without taking physical delivery.

4. **Options and Futures:** Derivative instruments that grant the right (options) or obligation (futures) to buy or sell an underlying asset at a predetermined price and date. These instruments are commonly used for hedging and speculation.

5. **Bonds:** Trading debt securities issued by governments, corporations, or municipalities. Bond trading involves lending money to the issuer in exchange for periodic interest payments and the return of the principal amount at maturity.

6. **Cryptocurrencies:** Trading digital assets like Bitcoin, Ethereum, and others on cryptocurrency exchanges. Cryptocurrency trading is known for its 24/7 availability and high volatility.

Trading Styles and Strategies

Trading encompasses various styles and strategies tailored to meet the goals and risk tolerance of individual traders:

1. **Day Trading:** Day traders buy and sell assets within the same trading day, aiming to profit from short-term price fluctuations. They often use technical analysis and chart patterns.

2. **Swing Trading:** Swing traders hold positions for several days to weeks, capitalizing on medium-term price swings. They may rely on both technical and fundamental analysis.

3. **Position Trading:** Position traders have a longer-term horizon, holding positions for weeks, months, or even years. They often focus on fundamental analysis and macroeconomic trends.

4. **Scalping:** Scalpers aim to profit from small price movements by executing a large number of trades in a short time frame. They rely on technical analysis and fast execution.

5. **Algorithmic Trading:** Algorithmic or algo traders use computer algorithms to execute trades automatically based on predefined criteria or signals. Algo trading is prevalent in high-frequency trading and quantitative strategies.

Risk and Reward in Trading

Trading offers the potential for significant rewards, but it comes with inherent risks. The market's unpredictability, leverage, and the emotional aspect of decision-making make trading a challenging endeavor. It is essential for traders to manage risk through techniques such as stop-loss orders, risk-reward analysis, and diversification.

TYPES OF TRADERS IN THE FINANCIAL MARKETS

There are several types of traders in the financial markets, each with a unique approach and time horizon for their trades. Here are some common types of traders:

1. **Day Traders:** Day traders buy and sell financial instruments within the same trading day. They aim to profit from short-term price fluctuations and typically do not hold positions overnight.

2. **Swing Traders:** Swing traders hold positions for several days to weeks, aiming to capture short to medium-term price movements. They rely on technical and fundamental analysis.

3. **Position Traders:** Position traders have a long-term perspective and may hold positions for weeks, months, or even years. They base their decisions on fundamental analysis and macroeconomic factors.

4. **Scalpers:** Scalpers are ultra-short-term traders who make numerous trades throughout the day, aiming to profit from tiny price movements. They often focus on high liquidity and tight spreads.

5. **Algorithmic Traders:** Algorithmic traders use computer algorithms and automated trading systems to execute trades based on predefined criteria. These traders can engage in various strategies, including arbitrage and trend following.

6. **High-Frequency Traders (HFTs):** HFTs are a subset of algorithmic traders who execute a large number of trades in fractions of a second. They often rely on high-speed data feeds and complex algorithms to profit from small price differentials.

7. **Quantitative Traders:** Quantitative traders use mathematical models and statistical analysis to develop trading strategies. They may employ a combination of fundamental and technical factors.

8. **Event-Driven Traders:** Event-driven traders focus on specific events, such as earnings announcements, mergers, or economic releases. They aim to profit from the price volatility generated by these events.

9. **Arbitrageurs:** Arbitrageurs seek to profit from price discrepancies between related assets or markets. They simultaneously buy and sell assets to capture risk-free profits.

10. **Social Traders:** Social traders use social trading platforms to follow and replicate the trades of experienced traders. They may base their decisions on the performance and strategies of others.

11. **Copy Traders:** Copy traders mimic the trades of successful investors or traders. They automatically replicate the trades made by their chosen trading mentors.

12. **Options Traders:** Options traders specialize in trading options contracts, which provide them with the right (but not the obligation) to buy or sell an underlying asset at a predetermined price.

13. **Commodity Traders:** Commodity traders focus on buying and selling physical commodities such as gold, oil, and agricultural products. They may trade futures contracts or physical commodities.

14. **Forex Traders:** Forex traders engage in the foreign exchange market, where they trade currency pairs with the goal of profiting from changes in exchange rates.

15. **Cryptocurrency Traders:** Cryptocurrency traders buy and sell cryptocurrencies like Bitcoin, Ethereum, and others. They aim to profit from the price volatility in the crypto market.

These are some of the primary types of traders you may encounter in the financial markets. Traders often choose their style based on their risk tolerance, time availability, and the strategies that align with their goals.

TRADING SURVIVAL TECHNIQUES

Trading survival techniques are strategies and practices that traders employ to navigate the challenges of the financial markets and increase their chances of long-term success. Surviving and thriving in trading requires more than just knowledge of the markets; it involves discipline, risk management, and psychological resilience. Here are some essential trading survival techniques:

1. **Risk Management:** Protecting your capital is paramount. Use stop-loss orders to limit potential losses on each trade. Never risk more than you can afford to lose in a single trade or overall.

2. **Position Sizing:** Determine the appropriate position size for each trade based on your risk tolerance and account size. Avoid over-leveraging, which can lead to significant losses.

3. **Diversification:** Avoid putting all your capital into a single trade or asset. Diversify your portfolio across different assets or markets to spread risk.

4. **Trading Plan:** Develop a well-defined trading plan that outlines your entry and exit strategies, risk management rules, and trading goals. Stick to your plan consistently.

5. **Emotional Control:** Emotions like fear and greed can lead to impulsive decisions. Practice emotional control by sticking to your trading plan and avoiding impulsive trades.

6. **Continuous Learning:** Stay updated with market trends, trading strategies, and economic events. The more knowledge you have, the better equipped you'll be to make informed decisions.

7. **Journaling:** Maintain a trading journal to record your trades, thoughts, and emotions. Regularly review your journal to identify patterns and areas for improvement.

8. **Adaptability:** Markets change, and successful traders adapt. Be open to adjusting your strategies and tactics based on changing market conditions.

9. **Patience:** Avoid rushing into trades. Wait for high-probability setups that align with your trading plan. Patience can prevent impulsive and costly mistakes.

10. **Continuous Assessment:** Regularly assess your trading performance. Analyze your wins and losses to identify strengths and weaknesses.

11. **Risk-Reward Ratio:** Always consider the risk-reward ratio before entering a trade. Ensure that potential profits justify the potential losses.

12. **Leverage Caution:** If you use leverage, do so with caution. High leverage can amplify both gains and losses, so it's essential to understand the risks involved.

13. **Stay Informed:** Keep an eye on economic calendars, news releases, and events that could impact the markets. Being well-informed helps you make timely decisions.

14. **Avoid Revenge Trading:** After a losing trade, avoid the temptation to chase losses by making impulsive trades to recover. Stick to your plan.

15. **Mental Resilience:** Develop mental resilience to handle losses and setbacks. Understand that losses are part of trading and use them as opportunities for learning and improvement.

16. **Take Breaks:** Trading can be intense. Take regular breaks to clear your mind and reduce stress.

17. **Community and Mentorship:** Join trading communities or seek mentorship from experienced traders. Learning from others' experiences can be invaluable.

18. **Goal Setting:** Set clear and achievable trading goals. Having objectives can help you stay focused and motivated.

19. **Exit Strategy:** Determine in advance when you will exit a winning or losing trade. Avoid making emotional decisions in the heat of the moment.

20. **Simulated Trading:** If you're new to trading or trying out a new strategy, consider using a demo or paper trading account to practice without risking real money.

Trading survival techniques encompass both technical skills and psychological resilience. Developing a structured approach to trading, managing risk effectively, and maintaining emotional discipline are critical to long-term success in the markets.

FUTURES IN TRADING

Futures trading is a cornerstone of financial markets, offering traders a unique opportunity to speculate on the future price movements of various assets, including commodities, currencies, stock market indices, and more. In this chapter, we will delve into the world of futures trading, exploring its fundamental concepts, mechanics, and providing real-world examples to illustrate its role and significance in the financial industry.

Understanding Futures Contracts:

A futures contract is a standardized financial agreement between two parties, where one agrees to buy, and the other agrees to sell a specific quantity of an underlying asset at a predetermined price on a specified future date. Futures contracts serve several essential functions in the financial markets:

1. **Price Discovery:** Futures markets play a crucial role in price discovery. They provide a transparent platform where supply and demand factors interact to determine future prices for various assets.

Example: In the agricultural futures market, farmers and food processors use futures contracts to establish prices for crops like wheat and corn months before the harvest, providing price certainty for both parties.

2. **Risk Management:** Futures contracts allow hedgers, such as producers and manufacturers, to protect themselves against adverse price movements. By locking in future prices, they can shield themselves from the uncertainty of price fluctuations.

Example: Airlines may use futures contracts to hedge against rising fuel prices, reducing their exposure to fuel cost volatility.

3. **Speculation:** Traders and investors use futures contracts for speculative purposes. They aim to profit from price movements without the intention of taking physical delivery of the underlying asset.

Example: A trader speculates on the price of gold futures, hoping to profit from an anticipated increase in gold prices without ever intending to take possession of physical gold.

Key Features of Futures Contracts:

Futures contracts share several key features that distinguish them from other financial instruments:

1. **Standardization:** Futures contracts are highly standardized, specifying the quality, quantity, and delivery date of the underlying asset. This standardization ensures uniformity and transparency in the market.

2. **Leverage:** Futures trading typically involves a margin requirement, allowing traders to control a more substantial position with a relatively small upfront investment. However, leverage also amplifies both potential gains and losses.

3. **Mark-to-Market:** Futures contracts are marked to market daily. This means that the contract's value is recalculated daily based on the current market price. Profits or losses are settled daily between the parties.

4. **Expiration Dates:** Each futures contract has a predetermined expiration date when the contract is settled. Traders can choose to close their positions before expiration or take physical delivery of the underlying asset.

5. **Exchange-Traded:** Most futures contracts are traded on organized exchanges, providing a regulated and centralized marketplace with transparent pricing and counterparty risk management.

Example of Futures Trading:

Suppose a trader believes that the price of crude oil will rise in the coming months. They can enter into a long (buy) futures contract for one crude oil futures contract at $70 per barrel, with an expiration date in six months. The trader pays the initial margin, which is a fraction of the contract's total value.

Scenario 1: If, after six months, the price of crude oil rises to $80 per barrel, the trader can sell their futures contract at the current market price, realizing a profit of $10 per barrel (excluding transaction costs).

Scenario 2: Conversely, if the price of crude oil falls to $65 per barrel, the trader will incur a loss of $5 per barrel. This loss will be deducted from their margin account.

In both scenarios, the trader has the flexibility to close their position before the expiration date if they wish to realize their gains or limit their losses.

Conclusion:

Futures trading is a vital component of global financial markets, serving the needs of hedgers, speculators, and investors alike. These contracts provide a means to manage risk, discover future prices, and capitalize on price movements in a highly standardized and regulated environment. Whether used for portfolio diversification, speculation, or risk management, futures contracts play an integral role in shaping the dynamics of modern financial markets.

Chapter 8

How Trading Works

Trading is not merely about buying and selling financial instruments; it involves a complex interplay of market participants, strategies, and technologies. In this chapter, we will delve into the mechanics of how trading works, covering the key elements that drive market movements and decisions made by traders.

Market Orders and Limit Orders

Trading begins with the submission of orders, which specify the terms of a trade. The two primary types of orders are market orders and limit orders:

1. **Market Orders:** A market order is an instruction to buy or sell an asset at the current market price. Market orders are executed immediately, ensuring that the trade occurs promptly. These orders are typically used when traders prioritize speed of execution over price.

Example: Suppose you want to buy shares of a popular tech company, and the current market price is $100 per share. You submit a market order to purchase 100 shares. Your order is executed at the prevailing market price, and you acquire the shares at $100 each.

2. **Limit Orders:** A limit order, on the other hand, specifies a price at which a trader is willing to buy (limit buy order) or sell (limit sell order) an asset. These orders are not executed until the market reaches the specified price or better. Limit orders allow traders to control the price at which they enter or exit a trade but may not guarantee execution.

Example: Suppose you want to sell your shares of a stock currently trading at $150 per share. You place a limit sell order at $155 per share. Your order will only be executed if the market price reaches or exceeds $155.

Bid and Ask Prices

In a market, two key prices are constantly displayed: the bid price and the ask price.

1. **Bid Price:** The bid price represents the maximum price buyers are willing to pay for an asset at a given moment. It is the price at which market participants are looking to purchase the asset.

2. **Ask Price:** The ask price, also known as the offer price, is the minimum price at which sellers are willing to sell an asset. It is the price at which market participants are offering to sell the asset.

The difference between the bid and ask prices is known as the bid-ask spread. A narrower spread typically indicates higher liquidity in the market, while a wider spread may suggest lower liquidity and potentially higher transaction costs.

Order Book and Matching

Orders from market participants are aggregated in an order book, which displays the current bid and ask prices along with the respective quantities. The order book serves as a dynamic record of supply and demand in the market.

When a market order is submitted, it is matched with the best available opposite-side limit order in the order book. For example, if you submit a market buy order, it will be matched with the lowest ask price in the order book. Conversely, a market sell order will be matched with the highest bid price.

Price Discovery

Price discovery is a fundamental function of financial markets. It refers to the process by which market participants collectively determine the current market price of an asset based on supply and demand dynamics. As new information and trading activity occur, prices continuously adjust to reflect the latest consensus on an asset's value.

For instance, if a company releases better-than-expected earnings results, demand for its stock may surge, causing its price to rise. Conversely, negative news or events can lead to increased selling pressure and lower prices.

Market Participants and Liquidity

Market participants include a diverse range of actors, each with different motivations and trading strategies. They can be broadly categorized into:

1. **Retail Traders:** Individual investors who trade for personal or speculative purposes.

2. **Institutional Traders:** Large organizations, such as mutual funds, hedge funds, and pension funds, that trade on behalf of their clients or shareholders.

3. **Market Makers:** Financial institutions that provide liquidity to the market by continuously quoting bid and ask prices. They profit from the bid-ask spread.

4. **High-Frequency Traders (HFTs):** Automated trading firms that use algorithms to execute a high volume of trades at extremely high speeds. HFTs aim to profit from small price discrepancies.

5. **Arbitrageurs:** Traders who exploit price discrepancies between different markets or assets. Arbitrageurs seek risk-free profits by buying low and selling high in correlated markets.

6. **Speculators:** Traders who seek to profit from price movements by taking directional positions. They may employ technical or fundamental analysis to inform their trades.

Trading Technologies

Advances in technology have transformed the way trading is conducted. Electronic trading platforms have become ubiquitous, allowing traders to execute orders with speed and efficiency. These platforms provide access to a wide range of financial markets and instruments, enabling traders to make informed decisions, monitor their portfolios, and manage risk in real time.

Conclusion

Trading is a multifaceted process driven by market orders, limit orders, bid-ask prices, and an intricate web of market participants. Price discovery is at the heart of trading, as supply and demand dynamics continuously shape asset prices. Technology has revolutionized trading, providing traders with powerful tools and unprecedented access to global markets. In the chapters ahead, we will delve deeper into trading strategies, risk management techniques, and the psychological aspects of trading.

Chapter 9

Materials Required for Trading

Trading, like any other profession, requires specific tools and materials to operate effectively and make informed decisions. In this chapter, we will explore the essential materials needed for trading, whether you are a beginner or an experienced trader.

1. Capital:

Capital is the lifeblood of trading. It represents the money you use to buy and sell financial instruments. Depending on your trading style and risk tolerance, the amount of capital required can vary significantly. Adequate capital provides you with the ability to diversify your positions, manage risk, and take advantage of trading opportunities.

Example: If you have $10,000 in capital, you can allocate a portion of it to different trades, reducing your exposure to any single asset or market.

2. Trading Account:

A trading account is a specialized financial account that allows you to execute trades in financial markets. To open a trading account, you'll need to choose a brokerage firm that suits your needs and comply with their account opening requirements. Your trading account acts as a gateway to the financial markets.

Example: Online brokerage platforms like E*TRADE, Interactive Brokers, or Robinhood provide users with trading accounts to buy and sell stocks, options, and other assets.

3. Computer and Internet Connection:

A reliable computer and a high-speed internet connection are indispensable for online trading. You'll need a computer to access trading platforms, analyze market data, and execute trades. A fast and stable internet connection ensures that you can react quickly to market movements.

Example: Traders use desktop or laptop computers with trading software to monitor charts and execute trades. Mobile devices with trading apps provide flexibility for on-the-go trading.

4. Trading Software:

Trading software includes platforms and tools that enable you to analyze markets, place orders, and manage your trading activities. Many brokerages offer their proprietary trading platforms, while others support third-party software.

Example: MetaTrader 4 (MT4) and MetaTrader 5 (MT5) are popular trading platforms that provide charting, technical analysis tools, and order execution capabilities.

5. Market Data:

Accurate and up-to-date market data is crucial for making informed trading decisions. Market data includes price quotes, charts, news feeds, and other information relevant to the assets you're trading.

Example: Traders use market data to analyze price trends, identify potential entry and exit points, and stay informed about market events that may impact their positions.

6. Trading Strategy:

A trading strategy is a well-defined plan that outlines your approach to trading, including entry and exit criteria, risk management rules, and position sizing. Your trading strategy serves as a roadmap for making decisions in the market.

Example: A day trader might have a strategy that involves buying a stock when it breaks above its 20-period moving average and selling it when it falls below the 10-period moving average.

7. Risk Management Tools:

Risk management is a critical aspect of trading. You'll need tools and techniques to protect your capital and minimize losses. This includes setting stop-loss orders, using position sizing methods, and diversifying your portfolio.

Example: If you have a $10,000 trading account, you might limit your risk on each trade to 2% of your capital, which means you'll only risk $200 on any single trade.

8. Fundamental and Technical Analysis Resources:

Traders often rely on fundamental analysis (evaluating the intrinsic value of assets) and technical analysis (studying price charts and patterns) to inform their decisions. Access to financial news, research reports, and charting tools is essential.

Example: Traders use financial news sources like Bloomberg or Reuters for real-time news updates and technical analysis platforms like TradingView for chart analysis.

9. Trading Journal:

Maintaining a trading journal is a best practice for traders. It helps you record and review your trades, track performance, and learn from your successes and mistakes. A trading journal can be digital or physical.

Example: In a trading journal, you might record the date and time of each trade, the asset traded, entry and exit prices, reasons for the trade, and the outcome.

10. Trading Psychology Resources:

Trading psychology plays a significant role in success. Emotional discipline, stress management, and mental resilience are crucial for maintaining a clear and rational mindset while trading.

Example: Books like "Trading in the Zone" by Mark Douglas or courses on trading psychology can help traders develop the right mindset for trading.

11. Backup and Security Measures:

To safeguard your trading activities, it's essential to have backup systems, security measures, and contingency plans in place. Protecting your trading accounts and data from potential threats is vital.

Example: Traders use hardware security keys, strong passwords, and two-factor authentication (2FA) to enhance account security.

12. Continuous Learning Resources:

Trading is a dynamic field, and staying informed about market developments, trading strategies, and new technologies is crucial for ongoing success. Continuous learning resources include books, courses, webinars, and access to trading communities.

Example: A trader might enroll in a technical analysis course to improve their charting skills or participate in online forums to exchange ideas with other traders.

In conclusion, trading requires a range of materials, tools, and resources to be executed effectively. Whether you're a novice trader or a seasoned professional, having the right equipment and knowledge is essential for success in the dynamic world of financial markets. In the chapters ahead, we will delve deeper into trading strategies, risk management techniques, and the psychological aspects of trading.

Chapter 10

The Difference Between Investment and Trade

Investment and trade are two distinct approaches to participating in financial markets, each with its own objectives, strategies, and time horizons. In this chapter, we will explore the fundamental differences between investment and trade, highlighting their unique characteristics and the roles they play in wealth accumulation and financial planning.

Investment: Building Wealth Over Time

Definition: Investment involves allocating capital with the expectation of generating returns over an extended period. Investors focus on accumulating assets that appreciate in value, generate income, or both. Investment typically has a long-term horizon, often spanning years or decades.

Key Characteristics of Investment:

1. **Long-Term Focus:** Investors commit their capital with the expectation of holding assets for an extended period, allowing them to benefit from the power of compounding and the potential for long-term growth.

2. **Risk Tolerance:** Investors assess their risk tolerance and align their portfolios with their financial goals and comfort level. They are generally more willing to weather short-term market fluctuations.

3. **Diversification:** Diversification involves spreading investments across a range of asset classes (e.g., stocks, bonds, real estate) to reduce risk and enhance long-term returns.

4. **Income Generation:** Some investments, like dividend-paying stocks and bonds, provide regular income in the form of dividends, interest, or rental payments.

5. **Research and Analysis:** Investors often conduct thorough research and analysis to identify opportunities that align with their financial objectives and risk tolerance.

Example of Investment: Consider an individual who invests $10,000 in a diversified portfolio of stocks and bonds with the goal of funding their retirement in 30 years. They plan to hold these assets over the long term, reinvesting dividends and interest to benefit from compound growth.

Trade: Capitalizing on Short-Term Opportunities

Definition: Trade refers to the practice of buying and selling financial assets or instruments in the pursuit of short-term profits. Traders aim to profit from price movements that occur within hours, days, or weeks. Trading often involves higher frequency and more active management compared to investment.

Key Characteristics of Trade:

1. **Short-Term Focus:** Traders seek to capitalize on short-term price fluctuations, taking advantage of market inefficiencies or trends that may last only for a brief period.

2. **Risk Management:** Traders often employ risk management strategies such as stop-loss orders to limit potential losses and protect their capital.

3. **Technical and Fundamental Analysis:** Traders use technical analysis (examining price charts and patterns) and fundamental analysis (evaluating financial and economic data) to make short-term trading decisions.

4. **Leverage:** Some traders use leverage, which involves borrowing funds to amplify their trading positions. While it can magnify profits, it also increases the potential for losses.

5. **Active Monitoring:** Traders monitor markets closely, often making multiple trades within a single day or week. They may use trading platforms with real-time data and news feeds.

Example of Trade: A day trader buys 1,000 shares of a technology stock in the morning and sells them later the same day as the stock's price increases. The trader seeks to profit from the intraday price movement and is not concerned with the stock's long-term potential.

Key Differences Between Investment and Trade:

1. **Time Horizon:** Investment has a long-term focus, while trade is short-term and seeks to exploit immediate market opportunities.

2. **Risk Tolerance:** Investors typically have a higher risk tolerance for market fluctuations, while traders often have a lower tolerance and use risk management tools.

3. **Asset Selection:** Investors focus on building a diversified portfolio of assets for long-term growth, while traders select assets that align with their short-term trading strategies.

4. **Research Approach:** Investors conduct extensive research and analysis before committing capital, whereas traders may rely more on technical and short-term market signals.

5. **Frequency of Activity:** Investment involves less frequent buying and selling, whereas trade requires active monitoring and frequent transactions.

Investment and trade represent distinct approaches to wealth accumulation and financial participation in markets. Investors prioritize long-term growth and wealth preservation, while traders aim to capitalize on short-term opportunities. Understanding the differences between the two approaches is essential for individuals to align their financial goals, risk tolerance, and investment strategies effectively. individuals may choose to incorporate elements of both based on their unique circumstances and objectives.

Chapter 11

The Forex Market and Quotation

The Forex market, short for the foreign exchange market, is the largest and most liquid financial market in the world. It serves as the global marketplace for trading currencies, enabling participants to exchange one currency for another at determined exchange rates. Understanding how the Forex market operates and how currency quotations work is fundamental for anyone interested in international finance and trading.

The Forex Market: An Overview

The Forex market is decentralized, meaning it doesn't have a central exchange like the stock market. Instead, it consists of a vast network of financial institutions, including banks, corporations, governments, and individual traders, who engage in currency trading electronically. The primary purpose of the Forex market is to facilitate international trade and investment by providing a means to exchange one currency for another.

Currency Pairs: The Basis of Forex Trading

In the Forex market, currencies are quoted in pairs, reflecting the relative value of one currency against another. Each currency pair consists of two currencies: a base currency and a quote currency. The exchange rate tells you how much of the quote currency you need to buy one unit of the base currency.

Currency Pair Format:

- EUR/USD: Euro (EUR) is the base currency, and the U.S. Dollar (USD) is the quote currency.

- USD/JPY: U.S. Dollar (USD) is the base currency, and the Japanese Yen (JPY) is the quote currency.

Quotation Conventions

Currency pairs are quoted in two prices: the bid price and the ask price. The bid price represents the maximum price at which buyers are willing to purchase the base currency, while the ask price represents the minimum price at which sellers are willing to sell the base currency. The difference between the bid and ask prices is known as the spread.

Bid-Ask Spread Example:

- EUR/USD: Bid Price - 1.1000, Ask Price - 1.1002

- In this example, you can sell 1 Euro for 1.1000 USD (the bid price) or buy 1 Euro for 1.1002 USD (the ask price). The spread is 2 pips (0.0002).

Understanding Exchange Rates

Exchange rates in the Forex market are influenced by a variety of factors, including economic data, interest rates, geopolitical events, and market sentiment. Currencies are constantly traded 24 hours a day, five days a week, across major financial centers in different time zones, which means that exchange rates can fluctuate rapidly.

Major, Minor, and Exotic Pairs

The Forex market offers a wide range of currency pairs categorized into three main groups:

1. **Major Pairs:** These are the most frequently traded pairs and include currencies like the Euro (EUR), U.S. Dollar (USD), Japanese Yen (JPY), and British Pound (GBP).

2. **Minor Pairs (Cross-Currency Pairs):** These pairs do not include the U.S. Dollar as one of the currencies. Examples include EUR/GBP, AUD/JPY, and EUR/JPY.

3. **Exotic Pairs:** Exotic currency pairs involve one major currency and one from a smaller or emerging economy, such as USD/TRY (U.S. Dollar/Turkish Lira) or EUR/THB (Euro/Thai Baht).

Leverage and Margin in Forex Trading

Forex trading often involves the use of leverage, which allows traders to control larger positions with a relatively small amount of capital. While leverage can amplify profits, it also magnifies potential losses. Traders must manage leverage carefully and be aware of the margin requirements set by their brokers.

Conclusion

The Forex market is a dynamic and global marketplace where participants trade currencies in pairs. Understanding currency quotations and how exchange rates are determined is essential for anyone interested in Forex trading. The ability to navigate this market effectively involves staying informed about economic events, geopolitical developments, and market sentiment, as these factors can impact currency values and trading opportunities. Whether you are an individual trader, an institutional investor, or a multinational corporation, the Forex market offers a diverse array of currency pairs and trading strategies to suit your financial goals and risk tolerance.

Chapter 12

How to Make Money in Trading

Making money in trading is the primary goal for traders and investors in the financial markets. While trading can be highly profitable, it is also fraught with risks, and success is not guaranteed. In this chapter, we will explore the essential strategies and principles that can help traders increase their chances of making money in trading. We will provide practical insights, detailed explanations, and real-world examples to guide you on your trading journey.

Risk Management: The Foundation of Profitability

1. **Capital Preservation:** The first rule of making money in trading is not to lose it. Effective risk management is crucial. Determine how much capital you are willing to risk on a single trade, and set stop-loss orders to limit potential losses.

Example: A trader with a $10,000 trading account decides to risk no more than 2% of their capital on any single trade. This means they will not risk more than $200 on a trade.

2. **Position Sizing:** Adjust your position size based on your risk tolerance and the distance to your stop-loss. Smaller position sizes reduce risk and allow for more flexibility in managing trades.

Example: If you are trading a stock with a $5 stop-loss and are willing to risk $200, you can calculate your position size as $200 / $5 = 40 shares.

Trading Strategies and Analysis

3. **Technical Analysis:** Study price charts, patterns, and technical indicators to make informed entry and exit decisions. Technical analysis can help you identify potential trends and reversals in asset prices.

Example: Using moving averages to identify trend direction and using RSI (Relative Strength Index) to identify overbought or oversold conditions.

4. **Fundamental Analysis:** Evaluate the underlying factors that affect asset prices, such as economic data, company financials, and geopolitical events. Fundamental analysis can be especially important for long-term investing.

Example: Analyzing a company's earnings reports and economic indicators like GDP growth to make informed investment decisions.

Trading Styles

5. **Day Trading:** Day traders aim to profit from short-term price movements within a single trading day. They often make multiple trades in a day and avoid holding positions overnight.

Example: A day trader buys and sells a particular currency pair within minutes to hours, capitalizing on intraday price fluctuations.

6. **Swing Trading:** Swing traders aim to capture price swings over a few days to weeks. They rely on technical and fundamental analysis to identify potential entry and exit points.

Example: A swing trader enters a stock position after identifying a bullish trend reversal and holds the position for several days until the trend shows signs of exhaustion.

7. **Position Trading:** Position traders take long-term positions, holding assets for weeks, months, or even years. They often base their decisions on fundamental analysis.

Example: A position trader invests in a diversified portfolio of stocks with the intention of holding them for several years, aiming to benefit from long-term growth.

Continuous Learning and Adaptation

8. **Stay Informed:** Keep abreast of financial news and events that can impact the markets. Economic data releases, geopolitical developments, and central bank policies can have a significant influence.

Example: A trader monitors news regarding interest rate decisions by a central bank, as this can affect currency exchange rates.

9. **Learn from Mistakes:** Analyze your past trades, both winners and losers, to learn from your mistakes and successes. Adapt your trading strategy based on these insights.

Example: A trader reviews their losing trades and identifies a common pattern of impulsive decision-making, leading them to implement stricter discipline in their trading plan.

Conclusion:

Making money in trading is achievable with the right mindset, strategies, and discipline. Risk management is paramount to protect your capital, and choosing a trading style that suits your personality and goals is essential. Continuous learning, adaptation, and a commitment to improving your trading skills will help you increase your chances of success in the dynamic world of trading. While there are no guarantees in trading, a well-thought-out approach can lead to profitable results over time.

Here are key principles and attitudes that contribute to a successful trading mindset:

1. **Patience:** Successful traders understand that trading is not about making quick gains but rather about waiting for the right opportunities. Patience allows traders to avoid impulsive decisions driven by emotions.

2. **Discipline:** Discipline is the cornerstone of profitable trading. It involves following a well-defined trading plan, adhering to risk management rules, and not deviating from a strategy even in the face of losses.

3. **Emotional Control:** Emotions, such as fear and greed, can lead to irrational decisions. Winning traders keep their emotions in check, relying on logic and analysis rather than gut feelings.

4. **Continuous Learning:** The market is constantly evolving. Winning traders are committed to lifelong learning, staying updated on market news, and adapting to changing conditions.

5. **Risk Management:** Preserving capital is a top priority. Successful traders use proper position sizing, set stop-loss orders, and diversify their portfolios to manage risk effectively.

6. **Focus on Process, Not Outcomes:** Instead of fixating on the profit or loss of a single trade, successful traders focus on executing their trading plan consistently. They understand that outcomes can vary but that following a sound process will lead to long-term success.

7. **Adaptability:** Markets change, and winning traders adapt their strategies accordingly. They do not become attached to a single approach but remain flexible in response to shifting market dynamics.

8. **Mental Resilience:** Losses are part of trading, but they do not deter winners. They view losses as opportunities to learn and improve, rather than as personal failures.

9. **Goal Setting:** Setting clear and realistic trading goals helps traders stay motivated and focused on long-term success.

10. **Confidence:** Confidence in one's analysis and trading plan is crucial. However, overconfidence can be detrimental. Winning traders strike a balance between confidence and humility.

11. **Continuous Assessment:** Regularly reviewing and assessing one's trading performance is essential. This allows traders to identify strengths and weaknesses and make necessary adjustments.

12. **Risk-Reward Ratio:** Understanding the risk-reward ratio ensures that traders only take trades where potential profits outweigh potential losses.

13. **Diversification:** Spreading risk across different assets or markets can help protect a trading account from significant losses.

14. **Position Sizing:** Determining the appropriate position size for each trade based on risk tolerance and account size is a key aspect of risk management.

15. **Positive Mindset:** A positive attitude can help traders stay resilient during challenging periods. Positivity fosters a belief in one's ability to overcome obstacles.

16. **Record Keeping:** Keeping detailed records of trades, including entry and exit points, helps traders analyze their performance and make data-driven decisions.

17. **Trading Journal:** Maintaining a trading journal allows traders to document their thoughts, emotions, and observations, aiding in self-improvement.

18. **Acceptance of Responsibility:** Successful traders take full responsibility for their actions and decisions in the market, whether they result in profits or losses.

19. **Long-Term Perspective:** Rather than seeking short-term gains, winning traders have a long-term perspective. They understand that consistency and discipline lead to sustained profits.

20. **Continuous Improvement:** The best traders are always seeking ways to improve their skills and strategies. They view each trading day as an opportunity to refine their approach.

In summary, the winning market mentality that leads to profits is a combination of discipline, emotional control, adaptability, and continuous learning. Successful traders prioritize risk management, focus on process over outcomes, and maintain a positive and goal-oriented mindset. Developing these qualities and approaches can lead to sustained success in the trading world.

CHOOSING STOCKS TO TRADE

Choosing stocks to trade involves a systematic approach that takes into account various factors, including your financial goals, risk tolerance, and trading strategy. Here are steps to help you choose stocks to trade:

1. **Set Clear Goals:** Determine your investment objectives. Are you looking for long-term growth, regular income, or short-term gains? Your goals will influence your stock selection.

2. **Risk Tolerance:** Assess your risk tolerance honestly. How much volatility and potential loss can you handle without emotional distress? Your risk tolerance will help you choose the types of stocks to trade.

3. **Research:** Conduct thorough research on the companies you're interested in. Consider their financial health, competitive position, industry trends, and growth prospects.

4. **Market Analysis:** Analyze the broader market conditions. Look at economic indicators, interest rates, geopolitical events, and market sentiment. These factors can impact stock prices.

5. **Trading Strategy:** Decide on your trading strategy. Are you a day trader, swing trader, or long-term investor? Your strategy will determine your stock selection criteria.

6. **Fundamental Analysis:** Evaluate the fundamentals of a company. Look at earnings reports, revenue growth, profit margins, and debt levels. Assess if the company is undervalued or overvalued.

7. **Technical Analysis:** Use technical analysis to study stock price charts and patterns. Look for trends, support and resistance levels, and momentum indicators to time your trades.

8. **Diversification:** Don't put all your eggs in one basket. Diversify your portfolio by choosing stocks from different sectors and industries to spread risk.

9. **Liquidity:** Consider the liquidity of the stock. High liquidity means there are many buyers and sellers, reducing the risk of price manipulation.

10. **News and Events:** Stay informed about news and events related to the stocks you're trading. Earnings releases, product launches, and industry news can impact stock prices.

11. **Use Screeners:** Utilize stock screeners or trading platforms that offer screening tools to filter stocks based on your criteria.

12. **Risk Management:** Determine your stop-loss levels and profit targets before entering a trade. Stick to your risk management plan to limit losses.

13. **Paper Trading:** If you're new to trading or trying out a new strategy, consider paper trading or using a demo account to practice without risking real capital.

14. **Continuous Learning:** Stay updated with market trends, trading strategies, and financial news. Trading is an ongoing learning process.

15. **Review and Adjust:** Regularly review your trading performance and adjust your strategy as needed. Learn from both your successes and failures.

Remember that stock trading carries inherent risks, and there are no guarantees of profits. It's essential to have a well-thought-out trading plan and to stay disciplined in your approach. If you're uncertain about making trading decisions, consider seeking advice from a financial advisor or mentor.

Chapter 13

What Are Currency Pairs?

Currency pairs are the fundamental building blocks of the foreign exchange (Forex) market, where participants trade one currency for another. Understanding currency pairs is essential for anyone interested in Forex trading, as they represent the relative value of different currencies and play a pivotal role in global finance. In this chapter, we will explore what currency pairs are, how they are structured, and their significance in the Forex market.

Definition of Currency Pairs:

A currency pair is a financial instrument that consists of two currencies, known as the base currency and the quote currency, presented in a specific format. The exchange rate of a currency pair indicates how much of the quote currency is needed to purchase one unit of the base currency.

Currency Pair Format:

- EUR/USD: Euro (EUR) is the base currency, and the U.S. Dollar (USD) is the quote currency.

- USD/JPY: U.S. Dollar (USD) is the base currency, and the Japanese Yen (JPY) is the quote currency.

Structure of Currency Pairs:

1. **Base Currency:** The base currency is the first currency listed in the pair, and its value is always equal to one unit. All exchange rate calculations are made in relation to the base currency.

2. **Quote Currency:** The quote currency is the second currency listed in the pair. It represents the value of the base currency in terms of the quote currency.

How Currency Pairs Work:

Currency pairs express the value of one currency in terms of another. When you see an exchange rate for a currency pair, it tells you how much of the quote currency is needed to buy one unit of the base currency. This rate is constantly changing as a result of market supply and demand dynamics.

Example: If the EUR/USD exchange rate is 1.1500, it means that 1 Euro (EUR) can be exchanged for 1.1500 U.S. Dollars (USD). Conversely, it would take 1.1500 USD to purchase 1 Euro.

Types of Currency Pairs:

Currency pairs can be categorized into three main groups:

1. **Major Pairs:** Major currency pairs are the most frequently traded pairs and include currencies from the world's largest economies. Examples include EUR/USD, USD/JPY, and GBP/USD.

2. **Minor Pairs (Cross-Currency Pairs):** Minor pairs do not include the U.S. Dollar as one of the currencies. They are often referred to as cross-currency pairs. Examples include EUR/GBP, AUD/JPY, and EUR/JPY.

3. **Exotic Pairs:** Exotic currency pairs involve one major currency and one from a smaller or emerging economy. These pairs are less liquid and may have wider spreads. Examples include USD/TRY (U.S. Dollar/Turkish Lira) or EUR/THB (Euro/Thai Baht).

Significance of Currency Pairs:

Currency pairs are at the core of Forex trading and international finance. They serve several crucial purposes:

1. **Facilitating Global Trade:** Currency pairs allow businesses and individuals to exchange one currency for another when conducting international trade and commerce.

2. **Price Discovery:** Exchange rates of currency pairs reflect market sentiment and economic fundamentals, helping participants assess the relative strength of different economies.

3. **Hedging:** Companies and investors use currency pairs to hedge against exchange rate fluctuations, reducing the risk of financial losses in international transactions.

4. **Speculation:** Traders and investors speculate on currency pairs to profit from price movements. They analyze technical and fundamental factors to make trading decisions.

5. **Economic Indicators:** Exchange rates of major currency pairs are influenced by economic indicators, such as interest rates, inflation, and economic growth, making them essential tools for economic analysis.

In summary, currency pairs are a fundamental concept in the Forex market, representing the relative value of different currencies. They play a pivotal role in global finance, serving as a means of exchange, a source of economic information, and a tool for risk management and investment. Traders and investors in the Forex market rely on their understanding of currency pairs to make informed decisions and navigate the complexities of international finance.

Chapter 14

Major Pairs and Cross Pairs in Forex Trading

In the world of Forex trading, currencies are quoted in pairs, and these pairs can be categorized into two main groups: major pairs and cross pairs. Understanding the distinctions between these two categories is essential for Forex traders, as it influences their trading strategies and market analysis. In this chapter, we'll delve into what major pairs and cross pairs are, their characteristics, and their significance in the Forex market.

Major Pairs:

Major currency pairs, often referred to simply as "majors," consist of currency pairs that include the U.S. Dollar (USD) as one of the currencies. These pairs are the most traded and liquid instruments in the Forex market due to the central role of the U.S. Dollar in international finance. Major pairs typically represent currencies from the world's largest and most influential economies. Some examples of major currency pairs include:

1. **EUR/USD:** Euro (EUR) against U.S. Dollar (USD)

2. **USD/JPY:** U.S. Dollar (USD) against Japanese Yen (JPY)

3. **GBP/USD:** British Pound (GBP) against U.S. Dollar (USD)

4. **AUD/USD:** Australian Dollar (AUD) against U.S. Dollar (USD)

5. **USD/CHF:** U.S. Dollar (USD) against Swiss Franc (CHF)

Characteristics of Major Pairs:

1. **High Liquidity:** Major pairs are the most heavily traded in the Forex market, resulting in narrow bid-ask spreads and high liquidity. This liquidity means that traders can enter and exit positions with ease.

2. **Market Sensitivity:** Major pairs are sensitive to global economic and political events, making them responsive to changes in interest rates, inflation, and economic growth in their respective countries.

3. **Low Spreads:** Due to their popularity and liquidity, major pairs often have lower spreads, making them cost-effective for traders.

4. **Abundant Information:** Traders have access to a wealth of information and analysis on major pairs, making it easier to conduct market research and analysis.

Cross Pairs (Minor Pairs):

Cross currency pairs, also known as "crosses" or "minor pairs," do not include the U.S. Dollar (USD) as one of the currencies in the pair. Instead, they represent the exchange rate between two major currencies other than the USD. Cross pairs can involve currencies from smaller or emerging economies and are often used by traders looking for diversification or specific trading opportunities. Examples of cross currency pairs include:

1. **EUR/GBP:** Euro (EUR) against British Pound (GBP)

2. **AUD/JPY:** Australian Dollar (AUD) against Japanese Yen (JPY)

3. **EUR/JPY:** Euro (EUR) against Japanese Yen (JPY)

4. **GBP/CHF:** British Pound (GBP) against Swiss Franc (CHF)

5. **NZD/CAD:** New Zealand Dollar (NZD) against Canadian Dollar (CAD)

Characteristics of Cross Pairs:

1. **Lower Liquidity:** Cross pairs generally have lower trading volumes compared to major pairs, which can result in wider bid-ask spreads and potentially increased trading costs.

2. **Specific Market Focus:** Traders who specialize in certain regions or have insights into particular currencies may find cross pairs attractive for their specific trading strategies.

3. **Diversification:** Cross pairs can provide traders with opportunities to diversify their portfolios and reduce risk by trading currencies not directly linked to the U.S. Dollar.

4. **Volatile Movements:** Due to lower liquidity, cross pairs can experience more significant price fluctuations and may exhibit greater volatility during certain market conditions.

In summary, major pairs and cross pairs are essential components of the Forex market, each offering unique opportunities and challenges for traders. Major pairs are characterized by their high liquidity, sensitivity to global events, and low spreads, making them popular choices for both beginner and experienced traders. Cross pairs, on the other hand, provide diversification options and specialized trading opportunities but may involve higher spreads and increased volatility. Traders should consider their objectives, risk tolerance, and market knowledge when choosing between major pairs and cross pairs for their Forex trading activities.

HERE'S A LIST OF SOME COMMONLY TRADED CURRENCY PAIRS IN THE FOREIGN EXCHANGE (FOREX) MARKET:

1. EUR/USD - Euro/US Dollar

2. USD/JPY - US Dollar/Japanese Yen

3. GBP/USD - British Pound/US Dollar

4. AUD/USD - Australian Dollar/US Dollar

5. USD/CAD - US Dollar/Canadian Dollar

6. USD/CHF - US Dollar/Swiss Franc

7. EUR/JPY - Euro/Japanese Yen

8. EUR/GBP - Euro/British Pound

9. NZD/USD - New Zealand Dollar/US Dollar

10. GBP/JPY - British Pound/Japanese Yen

11. EUR/AUD - Euro/Australian Dollar

12. USD/SGD - US Dollar/Singapore Dollar

13. USD/IIKD - US Dollar/Hong Kong Dollar

14. USD/INR - US Dollar/Indian Rupee

15. USD/MXN - US Dollar/Mexican Peso

16. EUR/CHF - Euro/Swiss Franc

17. EUR/CAD - Euro/Canadian Dollar

18. GBP/CHF - British Pound/Swiss Franc

19. GBP/AUD - British Pound/Australian Dollar

20. AUD/JPY - Australian Dollar/Japanese Yen

21. CAD/JPY - Canadian Dollar/Japanese Yen

22. AUD/NZD - Australian Dollar/New Zealand Dollar

23. EUR/NZD - Euro/New Zealand Dollar

24. EUR/USD - Euro/Canadian Dollar

25. EUR/TRY - Euro/Turkish Lira

26. GBP/SGD - British Pound/Singapore Dollar

27. AUD/CHF - Australian Dollar/Swiss Franc

28. NZD/JPY - New Zealand Dollar/Japanese Yen

29. CAD/CHF - Canadian Dollar/Swiss Franc

30. GBP/CAD - British Pound/Canadian Dollar

31. AUD/CAD - Australian Dollar/Canadian Dollar

32. GBP/NZD - British Pound/New Zealand Dollar

33. EUR/SEK - Euro/Swedish Krona

34. USD/SEK - US Dollar/Swedish Krona

35. USD/PLN - US Dollar/Polish Złoty

Please note that the Forex market offers a vast array of currency pairs, including major pairs, minor pairs, and exotic pairs. Major pairs involve the most traded currencies globally, while minor and exotic pairs involve currencies from smaller economies. Traders choose currency pairs based on their trading strategies, risk tolerance, and market conditions.

Chapter 15

What Is Market Structure?

Understanding market structure is essential for traders and investors seeking to navigate financial markets effectively. Market structure refers to the organization and mechanics of a market, including how orders are executed, the types of participants involved, and the dynamics that drive price movements. In this chapter, we'll explore the key components of market structure and their significance in trading, with examples to illustrate their practical implications.

1. Order Types:

Orders are the instructions traders use to buy or sell assets in the market. The primary order types include:

- **Market Orders:** These orders execute immediately at the current market price. Market orders are used when traders prioritize speed of execution over price.

- **Limit Orders:** Limit orders specify a specific price at which a trader is willing to buy (limit buy order) or sell (limit sell order) an asset. They are used to control the price at which a trade is executed.

- **Stop Orders:** Stop orders become market orders when a specified price level is reached. Stop-loss orders are used to limit losses, while stop-limit orders combine the features of limit and stop orders.

Example: A trader places a limit buy order for a stock at $50. If the stock's price drops to $50 or lower, the order will execute at $50 or better.

2. Market Participants:

Various types of market participants contribute to the structure of financial markets. These include:

- **Retail Traders:** Individual traders who trade for their personal accounts.

- **Institutional Traders:** Large financial institutions, such as mutual funds, hedge funds, and pension funds, that trade on behalf of their clients or portfolios.

- **Market Makers:** Market makers facilitate trading by providing liquidity. They buy and sell assets to ensure there is a market for them.

- **High-Frequency Traders (HFTs):** HFTs use advanced algorithms and technology to execute trades at extremely high speeds, often within microseconds.

- **Exchanges:** Organized marketplaces where assets are traded. Exchanges like the New York Stock Exchange (NYSE) or NASDAQ provide a structured environment for trading.

Example: An institutional trader representing a pension fund places a large buy order for a specific stock. Market makers and HFTs may participate by providing liquidity and executing trades.

3. Bid-Ask Spread:

The bid-ask spread represents the difference between the highest price a buyer is willing to pay (the bid) and the lowest price a seller is willing to accept (the ask). It is a key indicator of market liquidity and transaction costs.

Example: If the bid for a stock is $49.80, and the ask is $50.00, the bid-ask spread is $0.20. Traders who buy at the ask price and sell at the bid price incur a $0.20 cost per share.

4. Market Depth:

Market depth, also known as the order book, shows the cumulative number of buy and sell orders at different price levels. It provides insights into supply and demand dynamics in the market.

Example: A trader can observe the market depth to see that there are more buy orders (demand) at a particular price level, suggesting potential support for the asset's price.

5. Volume and Liquidity:

Trading volume represents the total number of shares or contracts traded in a specific period. Liquidity refers to the ease with which an asset can be bought or sold without significantly affecting its price.

Example: A stock with high trading volume and narrow bid-ask spreads is considered highly liquid, making it attractive to traders.

6. Market Orders vs. Limit Orders:

Market orders execute immediately but may result in slippage, where the actual execution price differs from the expected price. Limit orders offer control over execution prices but may not fill if the market doesn't reach the specified price.

Example: A trader places a market order to buy a stock at $50, but it executes at $50.10 due to rapid price fluctuations. Alternatively, a limit order at $50 may not execute if the stock's price doesn't reach that level.

In summary, market structure is a critical aspect of trading that influences order execution, participant behavior, and price dynamics. Traders must consider market structure factors when developing their strategies and managing risk. By understanding the intricacies of market orders, participant roles, bid-ask spreads, market depth, and liquidity, traders can make more informed decisions and navigate the complexities of financial markets effectively.

Chapter 16

What Is Forex?

Forex, short for the foreign exchange market, is the largest and most liquid financial market in the world. Also known as FX or currency market, Forex is the global marketplace for trading currencies, where participants buy, sell, exchange, and speculate on the value of one currency against another. This chapter will provide an in-depth understanding of Forex, its structure, participants, trading hours, and significance in the world of finance.

Structure of the Forex Market:

Forex operates as a decentralized market, meaning there is no single central exchange. Instead, it consists of a vast network of financial institutions, including banks, central banks, corporations, governments, hedge funds, and individual traders, who engage in currency trading electronically. The absence of a central exchange allows Forex to operate 24 hours a day, five days a week, across multiple time zones.

Currency Pairs:

At the heart of Forex trading are currency pairs, which represent the relative value of one currency against another. Each currency pair consists of two currencies: a base currency and a quote currency. The exchange rate of a currency pair tells you how much of the quote currency is needed to buy one unit of the base currency.

Example: In the EUR/USD currency pair, the Euro (EUR) is the base currency, and the U.S. Dollar (USD) is the quote currency. If the exchange rate is 1.1500, it means that 1 Euro can be exchanged for 1.1500 U.S. Dollars.

Participants in the Forex Market:

1. **Banks:** Commercial banks, central banks, and investment banks are major participants in the Forex market. They facilitate currency transactions for clients and engage in proprietary trading.

2. **Corporations:** Multinational corporations engage in Forex trading to manage currency risk related to international business operations and transactions.

3. **Hedge Funds and Investment Firms:** These institutions engage in Forex trading to seek profit opportunities, often using various strategies, including algorithmic trading.

4. **Retail Traders:** Individuals participate in the Forex market through retail brokers. Retail traders can access the market with relatively small amounts of capital, thanks to leverage provided by brokers.

Trading Hours:

Forex operates 24 hours a day, five days a week, due to the global nature of the market and the presence of major financial centers in different time zones. The market is divided into three main trading sessions:

1. **Asian Session:** This session starts in Tokyo and overlaps with the Sydney session. It accounts for a significant portion of Forex trading volume.

2. **European Session:** The London session is the most active and liquid, with significant trading volume. It overlaps with the Asian and North American sessions.

3. **North American Session:** The New York session is the final major session and often experiences high volatility as it overlaps with the European session.

Significance of Forex:

Forex plays a pivotal role in the global economy and financial markets for several reasons:

1. **Facilitating International Trade:** Forex enables businesses to convert one currency into another, facilitating cross-border trade and commerce.

2. **Speculation and Investment:** Forex offers opportunities for traders and investors to speculate on currency price movements and generate returns through trading strategies.

3. **Hedging:** Companies and investors use Forex to hedge against currency risk, protecting themselves from adverse exchange rate movements.

4. **Economic Indicators:** Exchange rates in Forex are influenced by economic indicators such as interest rates, inflation, and economic growth, making them essential tools for economic analysis.

5. **Liquidity and Accessibility:** Forex is highly liquid, meaning that participants can enter and exit positions with ease. Retail traders can access the market through online brokers.

In summary, Forex is a dynamic and global marketplace for currency trading, where participants exchange and speculate on the value of currencies. It serves as a vital component of the global financial system, facilitating international trade, providing investment opportunities, and influencing economic decisions worldwide. Traders and investors involved in Forex must understand its structure, currency pairs, participants, trading hours, and significance to navigate this complex and exciting financial market effectively.

Chapter 17

Forex Terminology

Forex, as a specialized financial market, comes with its own unique set of terminology and jargon. Understanding these terms is essential for traders and investors to communicate effectively and navigate the complexities of currency trading. In this chapter, we will explore key Forex terminology, providing detailed explanations and examples to enhance your comprehension.

1. Pips:

A pip, short for "percentage in point" or "price interest point," is the smallest price move that a currency exchange rate can make based on market convention. Most currency pairs are quoted to four or five decimal places, and a pip represents the change in the last digit of the exchange rate.

Example: If the EUR/USD exchange rate moves from 1.1500 to 1.1501, it has moved up by one pip.

2. Lot Size:

Lot size refers to the standardized quantity of currency units in a Forex trade. The two common lot sizes are:

- **Standard Lot:** 100,000 units of the base currency.

- **Mini Lot:** 10,000 units of the base currency.

Example: If you open a trade with one standard lot of EUR/USD, you are trading 100,000 Euros.

3. Leverage:

Leverage allows traders to control a large position with a relatively small amount of capital. It is expressed as a ratio (e.g., 50:1), indicating the amount of borrowed funds compared to the trader's own capital.

Example: With 50:1 leverage, you can control a $50,000 position with only $1,000 of your own capital.

4. Margin:

Margin is the amount of money required to open and maintain a leveraged position. It is a percentage of the total position size and serves as collateral to cover potential losses.

Example: If you trade one standard lot of EUR/USD with a 2% margin requirement, you would need $2,000 in your account as margin.

5. Long and Short Positions:

- **Long Position:** Buying a currency pair with the expectation that its value will rise. In a long position, you profit from an increase in the exchange rate.

- **Short Position:** Selling a currency pair with the expectation that its value will fall. In a short position, you profit from a decrease in the exchange rate.

Example: If you believe the EUR/USD will rise, you take a long position by buying the pair. If you expect it to fall, you take a short position by selling it.

6. Spread:

The spread is the difference between the bid price (the price at which you can sell) and the ask price (the price at which you can buy) in a currency pair. It represents the transaction cost in Forex trading.

Example: If the EUR/USD has a bid price of 1.1500 and an ask price of 1.1502, the spread is 2 pips.

7. Currency Pair Notation:

Currency pairs are represented in standardized notation, with the base currency listed first, followed by the quote currency.

Example: In USD/JPY, the U.S. Dollar (USD) is the base currency, and the Japanese Yen (JPY) is the quote currency.

8. Stop-Loss Order:

A stop-loss order is a predetermined price level at which a trader specifies to close a losing position automatically, limiting potential losses.

Example: If you enter a long position on EUR/USD at 1.1500 and set a stop-loss order at 1.1450, your position will be automatically closed if the price reaches 1.1450, limiting your loss to 50 pips.

9. Take-Profit Order:

A take-profit order is a pre-defined price level at which a trader specifies to close a winning position automatically, locking in profits.

Example: If you enter a long position on EUR/USD at 1.1500 and set a take-profit order at 1.1550, your position will be automatically closed if the price reaches 1.1550, securing a profit of 50 pips.

10. Liquidity:

Liquidity refers to the ease with which a currency pair can be bought or sold without significantly affecting its price. Major pairs typically have high liquidity, while exotic pairs may have lower liquidity.

Example: EUR/USD is considered highly liquid, as large trading volumes ensure that you can easily execute trades without causing substantial price movements.

11. Fundamental Analysis and Technical Analysis:

- **Fundamental Analysis:** Examining economic, political, and financial data to assess a currency pair's intrinsic value and potential future movements.

- **Technical Analysis:** Analyzing historical price charts, patterns, and technical indicators to forecast future price movements.

Example: A trader may use fundamental analysis to assess a country's economic health and interest rates before making a trading decision. Alternatively, they might use technical analysis to identify support and resistance levels on a price chart.

Understanding these Forex terms is crucial for traders and investors to communicate effectively and make informed decisions. Whether you are a novice or an experienced trader, mastering these fundamental concepts will enhance your ability to navigate the dynamic world of currency trading.

Here is a long list of Forex terminology commonly used in the foreign exchange market:

1. Ask Price: The price at which a trader can buy a currency pair.

2. Bid Price: The price at which a trader can sell a currency pair.

3. Spread: The difference between the bid and ask price.

4. Pip: The smallest price movement in a currency pair, usually the fourth decimal place.

5. Lot: A standardized trading size. Standard lot size is 100,000 units of the base currency.

6. Mini Lot: A smaller lot size, typically 10,000 units of the base currency.

7. Micro Lot: An even smaller lot size, typically 1,000 units of the base currency.

8. Leverage: Borrowed capital used to amplify potential profits (or losses) in trading.

9. Margin: The amount of money required to open and maintain a trading position.

10. Margin Call: A request for additional funds to cover trading losses.

11. Stop-Loss Order: An order placed to limit potential losses by selling a position at a specified price.

12. Take-Profit Order: An order placed to lock in profits by selling a position at a specified price.

13. Market Order: An order to buy or sell a currency pair at the current market price.

14. Limit Order: An order to buy or sell a currency pair at a specified price or better.

15. Stop Order: An order to buy or sell a currency pair when it reaches a specified price.

16. Entry Order: An order to open a position at a specific price.

17. Exit Order: An order to close a position at a specific price.

18. Long Position: Buying a currency pair with the expectation that it will appreciate.

19. Short Position: Selling a currency pair with the expectation that it will depreciate.

20. Base Currency: The first currency in a currency pair.

21. Quote Currency: The second currency in a currency pair.

22. Major Pairs: Currency pairs that include the US Dollar (e.g., EUR/USD, USD/JPY).

23. Cross Pairs: Currency pairs that do not include the US Dollar (e.g., EUR/GBP, AUD/JPY).

24. Exotic Pairs: Currency pairs involving one major currency and one less common currency (e.g., USD/TRY, EUR/SGD).

25. Bull Market: A market characterized by rising prices.

26. Bear Market: A market characterized by falling prices.

27. Liquidity: The ease with which an asset can be bought or sold without significantly affecting its price.

28. Volatility: The degree of price fluctuations in a currency pair.

29. Fundamental Analysis: Analyzing economic, political, and social factors to predict currency price movements.

30. Technical Analysis: Analyzing historical price and volume data to predict currency price movements.

31. Support Level: A price level at which a currency pair tends to find buying interest.

32. Resistance Level: A price level at which a currency pair tends to encounter selling pressure.

33. Carry Trade: A strategy involving borrowing funds in a currency with a low-interest rate and investing in a currency with a higher interest rate.

34. Risk-On: A market sentiment where traders are willing to take on higher-risk investments.

35. Risk-Off: A market sentiment where traders seek safety in low-risk assets.

36. Forex Broker: A financial institution or platform that facilitates currency trading.

37. Slippage: The difference between the expected price of a trade and the actual execution price.

38. Rollover or Swap Rate: The interest rate differential between two currencies in a currency pair.

39. Volatility Index (VIX): A measure of market volatility and investor sentiment.

40. Economic Calendar: A schedule of economic events and announcements that can impact currency prices.

41. Carry Cost: The cost associated with holding a position overnight.

42. Central Bank: A government or quasi-governmental institution responsible for monetary policy.

43. Bullish: An optimistic outlook on a currency pair, expecting it to rise in value.

44. Bearish: A pessimistic outlook on a currency pair, expecting it to fall in value.

45. Fibonacci Retracement: A technical analysis tool used to identify potential support and resistance levels.

46. Moving Average: A trend-following indicator that smooths out price data to identify trends.

47. Oscillator: A technical indicator that oscillates between fixed levels to identify overbought or oversold conditions.

48. Stochastic Oscillator: A momentum indicator that measures the relative position of a currency's closing price within a trading range.

49. Relative Strength Index (RSI): A momentum oscillator that measures the speed and change of price movements.

50. MACD (Moving Average Convergence Divergence): A trend-following momentum indicator that shows the relationship between two moving averages.

51. Fibonacci Levels: Key levels based on Fibonacci ratios, often used for identifying support and resistance levels.

52. Candlestick Chart: A chart that displays price data using candlestick patterns to visualize price movements.

53. Bullish Engulfing Pattern: A candlestick pattern where a small bearish candle is followed by a larger bullish candle.

54. Bearish Engulfing Pattern: A candlestick pattern where a small bullish candle is followed by a larger bearish candle.

55. Hammer: A bullish reversal candlestick pattern characterized by a small body and long lower shadow.

56. Doji: A candlestick pattern indicating market indecision, often signaling a potential reversal.

57. Triangle Pattern: A technical analysis pattern formed by converging trendlines, indicating a potential breakout.

58. Head and Shoulders: A reversal pattern with three peaks, often signaling a trend reversal.

59. Risk-Reward Ratio: The ratio of potential profit to potential loss in a trade.

60. Drawdown: The decline in a trader's account balance from its peak value.

Chapter 18

Pip Value Calculation

In Forex trading, understanding pip value is a fundamental aspect of risk management and profit calculation. A pip, which stands for "percentage in point" or "price interest point," is the smallest price move a currency exchange rate can make based on market convention. Pip value helps traders determine the monetary value of each pip movement in their positions, allowing for precise position sizing and profit/loss assessment. In this chapter, we will delve into how pip value is calculated and why it is crucial for Forex traders.

Pip Value Calculation for Different Lot Sizes:

The formula for calculating pip value depends on the lot size you are trading. The three most common lot sizes are:

1. **Standard Lot:** 100,000 units of the base currency.

2. **Mini Lot:** 10,000 units of the base currency.

3. **Micro Lot:** 1,000 units of the base currency.

Pip Value for Standard Lots:

The formula for calculating pip value for standard lots is straightforward:

Pip Value = (0.0001 / Exchange Rate) x Trade Size

- 0.0001 represents one pip in most currency pairs (exception: JPY pairs, where it is 0.01).

- Exchange Rate is the current exchange rate of the currency pair.

- Trade Size is the number of standard lots traded.

Example: Let's say you are trading one standard lot of EUR/USD with an exchange rate of 1.1500. Using the formula:

Pip Value = (0.0001 / 1.1500) x 100,000 = $8.70

In this example, each pip movement in the EUR/USD pair is worth $8.70.

Pip Value for Mini Lots:

For mini lots, the formula is the same but with the trade size adjusted for mini lots:

Pip Value = (0.0001 / Exchange Rate) x (Trade Size / 10,000)

Example: Trading one mini lot of GBP/JPY at an exchange rate of 152.50:

Pip Value = (0.01 / 152.50) x (10,000 / 10,000) = $0.0656

In this case, each pip movement in the GBP/JPY pair is worth $0.0656.

Pip Value for Micro Lots:

The pip value calculation for micro lots is also similar, with the trade size adjusted for micro lots:

Pip Value = (0.0001 / Exchange Rate) x (Trade Size / 1,000)

Example: Trading three micro lots of AUD/USD at an exchange rate of 0.7500:

Pip Value = (0.0001 / 0.7500) x (3,000 / 1,000) = $0.04

Here, each pip movement in the AUD/USD pair is worth $0.04.

Significance of Pip Value:

Understanding pip value is crucial for Forex traders for several reasons:

1. **Position Sizing:** Knowing the value of each pip allows traders to determine the appropriate position size based on their risk tolerance and account size.

2. **Risk Management:** Calculating pip value helps traders set stop-loss and take-profit levels to manage risk effectively.

3. **Profit and Loss Calculation:** Traders can assess potential profits and losses by considering pip movements and position size.

4. **Currency Pair Comparison:** Traders can compare the value of pips

5. align with their risk-reward preferences.

In summary, pip value calculation is an essential skill for Forex traders, enabling them to make informed decisions about position sizing, risk management, and profit potential. By understanding how pip value varies with different lot sizes and currency pairs, traders can better navigate the dynamic and high-stakes world of Forex trading.

WHAT IS A PIPETTE?

In trading, a "pipette" is a fractional unit of a pip, which is the smallest price movement that can occur in the exchange rate of a currency pair. While a standard pip represents a one-unit change in the fourth decimal place for most currency pairs (except for Japanese yen pairs), a pipette represents a movement of 1/10th of a pip.

To provide some context, let's consider a few examples:

1. **Standard Pip:** In the EUR/USD currency pair, if the exchange rate moves from 1.2000 to 1.2001, it has moved up by one pip.

2. **Pipette:** If the same EUR/USD exchange rate moves from 1.20001 to 1.20002, it has moved up by one pipette.

Pipettes are often used to provide more precise price quotes, especially in situations where traders need a higher level of accuracy for their analysis and trading decisions. Some brokers and trading platforms offer quotes with five decimal places (e.g., 1.20001), allowing for the representation of pipettes.

In practice, pipettes are particularly relevant in situations where traders are dealing with extremely tight spreads or are looking for precise entry and exit points in the Forex market. They help traders gauge smaller price movements that may not be visible when using standard pips.

WHAT IS A LOT?

In trading, a "lot" is a standardized unit of measurement used to quantify the size or volume of a trade. The lot size represents the number of units of a particular financial instrument or asset that you are buying or selling in a single transaction. Lot sizes can vary significantly depending on the type of asset being traded and the broker or exchange you are using.

Here are the common lot sizes for different types of assets in trading:

1. **Forex (Foreign Exchange):**

   - Standard Lot: 100,000 units of the base currency.

   - Mini Lot: 10,000 units of the base currency.

   - Micro Lot: 1,000 units of the base currency.

   - Nano Lot: 100 units of the base currency.

2. **Stocks:**

   - Lot size can vary depending on the stock and exchange but is typically a multiple of one share.

3. **Commodities:**

   - Lot sizes vary widely based on the commodity. For example, in gold trading, a standard lot is typically 100 troy ounces.

4. **Futures and Options:**

   - Lot sizes are standardized and determined by the exchange. For example, one E-mini S&P 500 futures contract represents a notional value of a certain dollar amount.

5. **Cryptocurrencies:**

- Lot sizes can vary by exchange and cryptocurrency but are often expressed in terms of the cryptocurrency itself (e.g., 1 Bitcoin, 10 Ethereum).

The choice of lot size in trading has implications for the risk and potential reward of a trade. Larger lot sizes can result in more substantial gains or losses, while smaller lot sizes allow for more precise risk management and position sizing. Traders select their lot sizes based on their risk tolerance, account size, and trading strategy.

It's essential to be aware of the lot size you are trading and how it affects your exposure to the market. Additionally, understanding lot sizes is crucial for calculating position sizes, setting stop-loss and take-profit levels, and managing risk effectively in your trading activities.

In trading, the term "future" typically refers to "futures contracts" or "futures trading." Futures contracts are standardized financial agreements that obligate the parties involved to buy or sell a specific quantity of an underlying asset (such as a commodity, financial instrument, or currency) at a predetermined price on a specified future date. Futures trading is a popular form of trading that occurs on organized exchanges and plays a crucial role in financial markets. Here are some key aspects of futures trading:

1. **Standardization:** Futures contracts are highly standardized, specifying the quantity and quality of the underlying asset, the expiration date, and the contract size. This standardization ensures uniformity and transparency in the marketplace.

2. **Leverage:** Futures trading typically involves the use of leverage, which allows traders to control a more substantial position with a relatively small upfront investment. While leverage can magnify potential gains, it also increases the risk of significant losses.

3. **Marketplaces:** Futures contracts are traded on organized and regulated futures exchanges, such as the Chicago Mercantile Exchange (CME) or the Intercontinental Exchange (ICE).

4. **Risk Management:** Futures contracts are used for various purposes, including hedging and risk management. Producers, manufacturers, and financial institutions use futures to protect themselves against adverse price movements.

5. **Speculation:** Many traders engage in futures trading for speculative purposes, aiming to profit from price movements in the underlying assets without any intention of taking physical delivery.

6. **Price Discovery:** Futures markets serve as price discovery mechanisms, where supply and demand interact to establish future prices for various assets. These markets provide transparency and facilitate fair value determination.

7. **Margin:** Futures traders are typically required to post an initial margin, which is a fraction of the contract's total value, as collateral. This margin is used to cover potential losses and is settled daily.

8. **Expiration:** Each futures contract has a predetermined expiration date when the contract is settled. Traders can choose to close their positions before expiration or take physical delivery of the underlying asset if they wish.

Futures trading is prevalent in various asset classes, including commodities (e.g., oil, gold, wheat), financial instruments (e.g., stock market indices, interest rates), and currencies (e.g., Forex futures). Traders use futures contracts to speculate on price movements, diversify portfolios, and manage risk. It's important to note that futures trading involves both opportunities and risks, and traders should have a solid understanding of the market, risk management, and the specific asset they are trading before engaging in futures trading activities

Chapter 19

Short Selling in Financial Markets

Short selling, often referred to simply as "shorting," is a trading strategy used in financial markets that allows investors to profit from the declining price of an asset. It is a fundamental concept in stock markets, but it is also applicable to other financial instruments like currencies, commodities, and derivatives. In this chapter, we will explore what short selling is, how it works, its risks, and provide real-world examples to illustrate its application.

Definition of Short Selling:

Short selling is a trading strategy where an investor borrows an asset, typically from a broker, with the intention of selling it at the current market price and repurchasing it later at a lower price. The goal is to profit from the price difference, benefiting from a falling market.

How Short Selling Works:

The process of short selling involves several steps:

1. **Borrowing the Asset:** The investor borrows the asset they want to short sell from a broker or another lender. This borrowed asset is usually sold immediately in the market.

2. **Selling the Asset:** After borrowing, the investor sells the borrowed asset in the market at the current market price. The proceeds from the sale are kept in a trading account.

3. **Waiting for Price Decline:** The investor waits for the price of the asset to fall, ideally creating a profit opportunity.

4. **Buying Back the Asset:** Once the price has declined to the desired level, the investor buys back the same asset from the market.

5. **Returning the Borrowed Asset:** The investor returns the purchased asset to the lender, completing the short sale transaction.

Example of Short Selling:

Let's illustrate short selling with an example involving a stock:

1. An investor believes that the shares of Company XYZ are overvalued and will decline in price.

2. The investor borrows 100 shares of Company XYZ from their broker.

3. These borrowed shares are immediately sold in the market at $50 per share, generating $5,000 in proceeds.

4. Over time, as anticipated, the price of Company XYZ shares falls to $40 per share.

5. The investor buys back 100 shares at $40 per share, spending $4,000.

6. The investor returns the 100 shares to their broker.

In this scenario, the investor made a profit of $1,000 ($5,000 initial proceeds - $4,000 repurchase cost), benefiting from the declining price of Company XYZ shares

Risks and Considerations:

While short selling can be profitable when executed correctly, it involves significant risks:

1. **Unlimited Losses:** Unlike buying an asset, where the maximum loss is the initial investment, short selling has unlimited loss potential if the asset's price rises significantly.

2. **Borrowing Costs:** Borrowing the asset comes with borrowing costs, including interest fees or dividends owed to the lender.

3. **Timing Risk:** Accurately timing the market and predicting price declines is challenging, as asset prices can be influenced by a wide range of factors.

4. **Margin Calls:** If the asset's price rises substantially, the broker may issue a margin call, requiring the investor to deposit additional funds to cover potential losses.

5. **Short Squeeze:** In some cases, a large number of short sellers covering their positions simultaneously can drive up the price of the asset, resulting in a short squeeze.

Despite these risks, short selling serves a vital role in financial markets by providing liquidity, price discovery, and opportunities for investors to profit from both rising and falling markets. However, it is a strategy that requires careful consideration, risk management, and a thorough understanding of market dynamics. Traders and investors should approach short selling with caution and employ appropriate risk-mitigation strategies.

Chapter 20

Brokers in Trading

Brokers are integral to the functioning of financial markets, acting as intermediaries that facilitate the execution of trades between buyers and sellers. They provide a bridge between individual or institutional traders and the various financial markets, offering access to a wide range of assets, from stocks and bonds to currencies and commodities. In this chapter, we will explore the role of brokers in trading, the different types of brokers, and their significance in the financial world.

The Role of Brokers:

Brokers play several critical roles in trading:

1. **Trade Execution:** Brokers execute buy and sell orders on behalf of their clients, ensuring that transactions are completed accurately and efficiently.

2. **Market Access:** Brokers provide access to financial markets, allowing traders to buy and sell assets that they may not have direct access to otherwise.

3. **Research and Analysis:** Many brokers offer research and analysis tools, reports, and expert advice to help clients make informed trading decisions.

4. **Risk Management:** Brokers often offer risk management tools such as stop-loss orders and limit orders to help clients protect their investments.

5. **Liquidity:** Brokers contribute to market liquidity by facilitating a large number of trades, ensuring that buyers and sellers can find counterparties.

Types of Brokers:

There are various types of brokers, each serving specific needs in the financial markets:

1. **Full-Service Brokers:** These brokers offer a wide range of services, including investment advice, research, portfolio management, and trade execution. They are often suitable for investors who prefer a hands-on approach and personalized guidance.

2. **Discount Brokers:** Discount brokers provide a streamlined and cost-effective platform for trading. They typically offer lower fees and commissions but may provide fewer research and advisory services compared to full-service brokers. They are popular among self-directed traders.

3. **Online Brokers:** With the rise of online trading, online brokers have become increasingly common. They offer web-based trading platforms, making it convenient for individuals to trade from anywhere with an internet connection.

4. **Forex Brokers:** These specialized brokers focus on the foreign exchange market (Forex) and provide access to currency trading. They offer various currency pairs for trading and often offer high leverage to Forex traders.

5. **Commodity Brokers:** Commodity brokers facilitate trading in commodities such as gold, oil, agricultural products, and metals. They are essential for traders and investors looking to diversify their portfolios with commodities.

6. **Stockbrokers:** Stockbrokers specialize in equities, allowing clients to buy and sell stocks listed on stock exchanges. They provide market research and investment advice tailored to individual stock trading.

The Broker-Client Relationship:

The relationship between brokers and their clients is built on trust, transparency, and communication. Clients rely on brokers to execute their orders efficiently, provide accurate market information, and safeguard their investments. In return, brokers earn commissions or fees for their services.

Examples of Broker Services:

- A full-service broker might offer personalized investment strategies and portfolio management services to high-net-worth clients.

- A discount broker provides a self-directed trader with a user-friendly online trading platform, access to research tools, and low-cost trade execution.

- A Forex broker offers traders access to the currency markets, providing a range of currency pairs and leverage options.

- A commodity broker facilitates the trading of futures contracts for agricultural commodities, energy products, or precious metals.

In conclusion, brokers are pivotal to the world of trading and investing, connecting traders and investors to the financial markets. Their services span a wide spectrum, catering to the diverse needs and preferences of market participants. Whether you seek guidance, research, or a cost-effective trading platform, choosing the right broker is a crucial decision that can significantly impact your trading experience and financial success.

Chapter 21

Be Aware of Scammers

While trading offers the potential for significant financial gains, it also attracts unscrupulous individuals and organizations looking to exploit the inexperienced and unsuspecting. Scammers in the trading world use various tactics to deceive, defraud, and steal from traders and investors. In this chapter, we will explore the common scams in trading, how to recognize them, and crucial steps to protect yourself from falling victim to these fraudulent schemes.

Common Trading Scams:

1. **Pump and Dump Schemes:** In this scheme, fraudsters artificially inflate the price of a stock or cryptocurrency through false or misleading information (pumping). Once the price rises significantly, they sell off their holdings (dumping), causing the price to crash and leaving unsuspecting investors with losses.

2. **Fake Trading Platforms:** Scammers create fake online trading platforms that appear legitimate but are designed to steal deposits and personal information from users. These platforms may promise guaranteed profits or offer fraudulent investment opportunities.

3. **Pyramid and Ponzi Schemes:** These scams involve recruiting new investors by promising high returns or guaranteed profits. Early investors are paid with funds from new investors, creating the illusion of a successful venture. Eventually, the scheme collapses, and most investors lose their money.

4. **Signal Services:** Some scammers claim to provide trading signals or advisory services that guarantee profitable trades for a fee. In reality, these signals are often worthless, and subscribers may incur significant losses.

5. **Phishing Scams:** Fraudsters send fake emails, messages, or websites that impersonate legitimate brokers, banks, or trading platforms. They aim to steal login credentials, financial information, or personal data.

6. **Investment Seminars and Courses:** Scammers may organize seminars, webinars, or courses that promise to teach trading secrets for a fee. These often turn out to be expensive and provide little to no valuable information.

How to Recognize and Avoid Scammers:

1. **Research and Due Diligence:** Before investing or trading, thoroughly research the broker, platform, or investment opportunity. Look for reviews, regulatory licenses, and any history of complaints or scams associated with them.

2. **Be Cautious of Guaranteed Profits:** If an offer sounds too good to be true, it probably is. Be skeptical of anyone promising guaranteed returns or risk-free investments.

3. **Check Regulatory Authorities:** Verify that the broker or platform is regulated by a reputable financial authority. Regulatory bodies vary by country, but they often provide a list of authorized entities on their websites.

4. **Avoid High-Pressure Sales Tactics:** Scammers may pressure you to make quick decisions or deposits. Take your time to evaluate any investment opportunity and consult with trusted advisors if needed.

5. **Be Wary of Unsolicited Offers:** Be cautious of unsolicited emails, calls, or messages offering trading advice or investment opportunities. Legitimate brokers and financial institutions do not typically initiate contact this way.

6. **Use Secure Connections:** Ensure that any website or platform you use for trading is secure. Look for "https" in the web address and use two-factor authentication when available.

7. **Educate Yourself:** The best defense against scams is knowledge. Educate yourself about the different types of scams and red flags to watch out for in trading.

Examples of Trading Scams:

1. *Pump and Dump Scam:* A group of fraudsters promotes a low-value stock as the next big investment opportunity through social media and spam emails. Unsuspecting investors buy the stock, driving up its price. The scammers then sell their shares at the inflated price, causing the stock to crash, and investors are left with significant losses.

2. *Fake Trading Platform:* An individual comes across an online trading platform that promises high returns with minimal risk. The platform asks for a deposit to open an account. After depositing funds, the investor realizes that they cannot withdraw their money, and the platform's customer support is unresponsive.

3. *Phishing Email:* An investor receives an email that appears to be from their broker, requesting verification of account details. The email contains a link to a fake website designed to steal the investor's login credentials.

In conclusion, the trading world offers many legitimate opportunities, but it also harbors scammers who seek to exploit unsuspecting traders and investors. Being aware of common trading scams, conducting thorough due diligence, and exercising caution can help protect you from falling victim to fraudulent schemes. Remember that if an offer seems too good to be true, it likely is, and it's crucial to prioritize your financial security by taking appropriate precautions.

Chapter 22

How to Choose a Broker?

Selecting the right broker is a critical decision for traders and investors. Your choice of broker can significantly impact your trading experience, access to markets, transaction costs, and the overall success of your trading endeavors. In this chapter, we will explore a comprehensive guide on how to choose a broker in trading, providing you with valuable insights and considerations to make an informed decision.

1. Regulatory Compliance:

One of the most crucial aspects when choosing a broker is ensuring they are regulated by a reputable financial authority. Regulatory bodies vary by country but often include organizations like the U.S. Securities and Exchange Commission (SEC), the Financial Conduct Authority (FCA) in the UK, and the Australian Securities and Investments Commission (ASIC). Regulatory oversight helps ensure that brokers follow strict standards of conduct, safeguard client funds, and provide transparent services.

2. Trading Instruments:

Consider the range of financial instruments the broker offers access to. Depending on your trading preferences, you may want access to stocks, bonds, forex, commodities, cryptocurrencies, or derivatives. Ensure that the broker provides access to the markets and assets you intend to trade.

3. Trading Platforms:

Evaluate the trading platforms provided by the broker. A user-friendly, reliable, and feature-rich trading platform can significantly enhance your trading experience. Most brokers offer web-based platforms, desktop applications, and mobile apps. Test out the platform's functionality, charting tools, order execution speed, and ease of use.

4. Transaction Costs:

Different brokers have varying fee structures. Be aware of transaction costs, including spreads (for forex), commissions (for stocks and options), and overnight financing charges (for CFDs and margin trading). Consider how these costs will impact your trading profitability over time.

5. Leverage and Margin Requirements:

If you plan to use leverage in your trading, understand the broker's leverage offerings and margin requirements. Be cautious with high leverage, as it can amplify both profits and losses. Ensure you are comfortable with the broker's margin rules.

6. Customer Support:

Accessible and responsive customer support is essential. Test the broker's customer service through various channels such as phone, email, and live chat. Assess their willingness and ability to address your inquiries and concerns promptly.

7. Research and Analysis Tools:

Depending on your trading style, access to research and analysis tools may be critical. Some brokers provide market research, economic calendars, technical analysis tools, and educational resources. These can be valuable for making informed trading decisions.

8. Security and Account Protection:

Check the broker's security measures to protect your funds and personal information. Reputable brokers use encryption technology to secure data transmission and may offer additional protections like segregated accounts to separate client funds from the broker's operational funds.

9. Account Types and Minimum Deposits:

Review the types of accounts the broker offers, including standard accounts, mini accounts, and premium accounts. Consider whether the broker's minimum deposit requirements align with your budget and trading goals.

10. Trading Hours:

Ensure that the broker's trading hours align with your preferred trading times and time zone. Some markets, like forex, operate 24/5, while others have specific trading hours.

11. Reviews and Reputation:

Research the broker's reputation by reading reviews from other traders and checking online forums. Pay attention to any negative feedback regarding withdrawal issues, trade execution problems, or unethical practices.

12. Demo Accounts:

Many brokers offer demo accounts that allow you to practice trading with virtual funds. Using a demo account can help you evaluate the broker's platform and your own trading strategies without risking real money.

Example of Choosing a Broker:

Suppose you are an aspiring forex trader looking for a reputable broker. You research several brokers and find Broker A, which is regulated by the FCA, offers a user-friendly trading platform, competitive spreads, and 24/5 customer support. Broker B, on the other hand, is not regulated, has higher spreads, and lacks research tools. You decide to choose Broker A due to its regulatory compliance, favorable trading conditions, and positive reputation among traders.

Chapter 23

Difference Between A-Book and B-Book Brokers

In the world of Forex trading, two common models of order execution exist: the A-Book model and the B-Book model. These models represent different ways brokers handle client orders and manage their exposure to market risk. Understanding the distinction between A-Book and B-Book brokers is essential for traders, as it impacts the quality of order execution, potential conflicts of interest, and the overall trading experience. In this chapter, we will delve into the differences between these two broker models, providing detailed insights and examples.

A-Book Brokers:

A-Book brokers, also known as Straight Through Processing (STP) or Agency brokers, operate as intermediaries between their clients and the broader market. They do not take the opposing side of client trades, but instead, they route client orders directly to liquidity providers such as banks, other brokers, or financial institutions. A-Book brokers earn their income through spreads and, in some cases, commissions.

Key Characteristics of A-Book Brokers:

1. **No Conflict of Interest:** A-Book brokers have no vested interest in clients' losses or profits since they do not act as counterparties to trades.

2. **Market-Driven Pricing:** Prices offered by A-Book brokers are typically derived from the interbank market, reflecting actual supply and demand dynamics.

3. **Transparency:** A-Book brokers often provide transparent order execution, allowing traders to see the actual market spreads and pricing.

4. **No Requotes:** Traders are less likely to experience requotes when trading with A-Book brokers, as orders are executed based on available market prices.

Example of A-Book Broker:

Suppose you place an order to buy 1 lot of EUR/USD with an A-Book broker. The broker routes your order to a liquidity provider, who matches it with another trader willing to sell 1 lot of EUR/USD at the prevailing market price. The broker earns a commission or spread markup on the transaction but does not take the opposing side of your trade.

B-Book Brokers:

B-Book brokers, also known as Market Makers, operate differently. Instead of routing client orders directly to the market, they act as counterparties to their clients' trades. This means that when clients buy, the broker sells, and when clients sell, the broker buys. B-Book brokers generate income from the spreads they offer clients and may also profit from clients' losses.

Key Characteristics of B-Book Brokers:

1. **Conflict of Interest:** B-Book brokers have a potential conflict of interest because they profit when clients lose money.

2. **Internalization:** B-Book brokers may choose to internalize client orders, matching them with other clients' orders internally rather than sending them to the broader market.

3. **Spreads and Slippage:** Prices offered by B-Book brokers may include wider spreads than those found in the interbank market, and traders may experience slippage during volatile market conditions.

4. **Risk Management:** B-Book brokers manage their exposure to client positions and market risk. They may offset client trades in the interbank market to hedge their exposure.

Example of B-Book Broker:

Suppose you place an order to buy 1 lot of EUR/USD with a B-Book broker. Instead of routing your order to the market, the broker takes the opposing side of your trade, effectively selling you 1 lot of EUR/USD from their own inventory. They profit from the spread and potentially your losses if the market moves against you.

Considerations for Traders:

Traders should be aware of the differences between A-Book and B-Book brokers when choosing a broker. Here are some key considerations:

- **Trading Style:** A-Book brokers may be preferable for scalpers and high-frequency traders who require tight spreads and fast execution. B-Book brokers may be suitable for longer-term traders who prioritize other factors like customer support or educational resources.

- **Conflict of Interest:** Consider whether you are comfortable trading with a B-Book broker that has a potential conflict of interest due to profiting from client losses.

- **Transparency:** Evaluate the transparency of order execution, pricing, and spreads offered by the broker.

- **Regulatory Compliance:** Regardless of the broker model, ensure the broker is regulated by a reputable financial authority to protect your funds and interests.

In conclusion, the distinction between A-Book and B-Book brokers is essential for traders to make informed decisions about their choice of broker. Each model has its advantages and disadvantages, and traders should consider their trading style, risk tolerance, and preferences when selecting a broker. Transparency, regulatory compliance, and understanding the broker's business model are crucial factors in ensuring a positive and secure trading experience.

Chapter 24

Understanding ECN Brokers and Commissions

In the world of online trading, Electronic Communication Network (ECN) brokers have gained popularity for their unique trading model that offers direct access to interbank markets. To navigate the complex landscape of ECN brokers and the associated commissions, traders need a comprehensive understanding of how these brokers operate and how commission structures can impact their trading costs. In this chapter, we will explore ECN brokers, commissions, and provide detailed insights along with real-world examples.

What Are ECN Brokers?

ECN brokers are financial intermediaries that connect retail traders directly to the interbank forex market. Instead of acting as counterparties to client trades, ECN brokers aggregate buy and sell orders from various participants, including banks, financial institutions, and retail traders. The ECN system then matches these orders based on the best available prices, offering traders access to a transparent and competitive marketplace.

Key Characteristics of ECN Brokers:

1. **Market Depth:** ECN brokers display market depth, allowing traders to see the available bid and ask prices along with the order sizes. This transparency provides valuable information about liquidity and potential price movements.

2. **Tight Spreads:** ECN brokers often offer tight spreads because prices are sourced directly from the interbank market. However, spreads can vary and may widen during periods of low liquidity or high market volatility.

3. **Direct Market Access:** Traders using ECN brokers typically experience faster execution and minimal slippage, as orders are executed based on real market prices.

4. **No Conflict of Interest:** ECN brokers do not take the opposing side of client trades, eliminating any conflict of interest. They earn their revenue through commissions and, in some cases, a small spread markup.

Understanding Commissions with ECN Brokers:

ECN brokers charge commissions as a primary source of income. The commission is usually based on the trading volume (lot size) and is applied to both the opening and closing of a trade. Commissions can be structured in different ways, including:

1. **Fixed Commissions:** Some ECN brokers charge a fixed commission per lot traded. For example, a broker may charge $5 per lot for a round-turn trade (both opening and closing positions).

2. **Variable Commissions:** In this model, the commission rate may vary depending on the trading volume. As traders execute larger trade sizes, they may receive volume-based discounts.

Example of ECN Broker Commissions:

Suppose you are trading with an ECN broker that charges a fixed commission of $5 per lot for forex trades. If you open a position of 2 lots of EUR/USD and then close it, you will be charged a total commission of $10 ($5 for opening and $5 for closing the trade).

Considerations When Trading with ECN Brokers:

1. **Total Trading Costs:** Traders should consider both spreads and commissions when evaluating the overall cost of trading with ECN brokers. While spreads are typically tight, commissions can add to the trading cost.

2. **Scalping and High-Frequency Trading:** ECN brokers are often favored by scalpers and high-frequency traders due to their fast

execution and transparency. However, frequent trading can lead to higher commission expenses.

3. **Trading Style:** Traders with longer holding periods may find ECN brokers cost-effective, while day traders and scalpers should assess the impact of commissions on their profitability.

4. **Regulatory Compliance:** Ensure that the ECN broker is regulated by a reputable financial authority to protect your funds and interests.

In conclusion, ECN brokers provide traders with direct access to interbank markets, offering transparency and competitive pricing. While ECN brokers charge commissions, traders benefit from tight spreads, fast execution, and minimal conflicts of interest. When choosing an ECN broker, it is essential to consider commission structures, trading style, and the overall trading cost to make informed decisions that align with your trading objectives.

Chapter 25

Different Methods of Analysis in Trading

Successful trading requires a deep understanding of market dynamics and the ability to make informed decisions. Traders employ various methods of analysis to gain insights into market trends, price movements, and potential opportunities. In this chapter, we will explore the three primary methods of analysis used in trading: fundamental analysis, technical analysis, and sentiment analysis, providing detailed explanations and real-world examples.

1. Fundamental Analysis:

Fundamental analysis involves examining the underlying factors that influence an asset's value, such as economic indicators, financial statements, news events, and geopolitical developments. This method aims to assess whether an asset is overvalued or undervalued based on its intrinsic worth. Fundamental analysts believe that by understanding these factors, they can make predictions about future price movements.

Key Aspects of Fundamental Analysis:

- **Economic Indicators:** Fundamental analysts examine economic data, including GDP growth, unemployment rates, inflation, and interest rates, to gauge the overall health of an economy and its impact on asset prices.

- **Corporate Performance:** When trading stocks, analysts evaluate a company's financial statements, earnings reports, and management performance to assess its growth potential and profitability.

- **Geopolitical Events:** Political stability, international relations, and major geopolitical events can significantly affect asset prices, especially in the forex and commodity markets.

Example of Fundamental Analysis:

Suppose you are considering trading the EUR/USD currency pair. You observe that the European Central Bank (ECB) has recently lowered interest rates due to weak economic data, while the U.S. Federal Reserve has hinted at raising interest rates due to strong economic growth. Based on this fundamental analysis, you anticipate that the USD may strengthen against the EUR, leading you to take a short position on the EUR/USD.

2. Technical Analysis:

Technical analysis focuses on analyzing historical price and volume data to identify patterns, trends, and potential price levels. This method assumes that historical price movements tend to repeat and that price charts contain valuable information about future price direction. Technical analysts use various tools and indicators to make trading decisions.

Key Aspects of Technical Analysis:

- **Chart Patterns:** Traders look for chart patterns such as head and shoulders, double tops, and triangles to identify potential trend reversals or continuations.

- **Indicators:** Technical analysts use indicators like moving averages, Relative Strength Index (RSI), and MACD to assess the strength and momentum of price movements.

- **Support and Resistance:** Support and resistance levels are price levels where an asset tends to find buying (support) or selling (resistance) pressure. Traders use these levels to set entry and exit points.

Example of Technical Analysis:

You are analyzing the price chart of a stock and notice that it has formed a "golden cross," where its 50-day moving average crosses above its 200-day moving average. This bullish technical signal suggests a potential uptrend, prompting you to consider a long position in the stock.

3. Sentiment Analysis:

Sentiment analysis focuses on gauging market sentiment and investor psychology. It involves assessing the collective sentiment of traders and investors through tools like news sentiment analysis, social media sentiment, and market positioning. Traders use sentiment analysis to understand whether market participants are bullish, bearish, or neutral on an asset.

Key Aspects of Sentiment Analysis:

- **News and Media:** Traders monitor news headlines and articles to gauge how news events and economic reports are affecting market sentiment.

- **Social Media:** Social media platforms like Twitter and Reddit can provide insights into retail trader sentiment and trends.

- **Market Positioning:** Tools like the Commitment of Traders (COT) report provide information about the positions of large institutional traders and commercials, helping traders gauge overall market sentiment.

Example of Sentiment Analysis:

You are considering trading a popular cryptocurrency, and you notice a surge in positive sentiment on social media platforms, along with a notable increase in trading volume. This may indicate a bullish sentiment among retail traders, prompting you to investigate potential long trading opportunities.

In conclusion, traders employ a combination of fundamental analysis, technical analysis, and sentiment analysis to make informed trading decisions. Each method provides a unique perspective on the market, allowing traders to assess different aspects of asset valuation and market sentiment.

Chapter 26

Technical Analysis vs. Fundamental Analysis

In the world of trading, two primary methods of analysis—technical analysis and fundamental analysis—serve as the cornerstone for making informed trading decisions. Traders and investors often debate which approach is more effective, but the truth is that both methods have their merits and are valuable tools when used appropriately. In this chapter, we will explore the key differences between technical analysis and fundamental analysis, providing detailed explanations, examples, and insights into their strengths and weaknesses.

Technical Analysis:

Technical analysis focuses on studying historical price and volume data to identify patterns, trends, and potential future price movements. It operates on the premise that past price behavior reflects all known information and that price movements tend to repeat or follow certain patterns. Here are the key aspects of technical analysis:

1. **Charts and Patterns:** Technical analysts use price charts to identify patterns such as head and shoulders, double tops, triangles, and more. These patterns are believed to provide clues about future price direction.

2. **Indicators and Oscillators:** Various technical indicators and oscillators, like moving averages, Relative Strength Index (RSI), and Moving Average Convergence Divergence (MACD), are employed to assess the strength and momentum of price movements.

3. **Support and Resistance:** Traders identify support levels (where buying interest tends to emerge) and resistance levels (where selling interest tends to surface) to set entry and exit points.

Example of Technical Analysis:

Consider a stock whose price has been trending upward for several months. A technical analyst might observe this uptrend on a price chart, notice that the stock consistently bounces off a rising trendline, and use this information to make a bullish trading decision.

Fundamental Analysis:

Fundamental analysis, on the other hand, involves evaluating an asset's intrinsic value by examining various factors, including economic indicators, financial statements, news events, and geopolitical developments. It aims to assess whether an asset is overvalued or undervalued based on its underlying fundamentals. Here are the key aspects of fundamental analysis:

1. **Economic Factors:** Fundamental analysts study economic indicators like GDP growth, unemployment rates, inflation, and interest rates to gauge the overall health of an economy and its potential impact on asset prices.

2. **Corporate Performance:** When analyzing stocks, fundamental analysts scrutinize a company's financial statements, earnings reports, and management performance to assess its growth potential and profitability.

3. **News and Events:** Fundamental analysis considers significant news events and geopolitical developments that can influence asset prices, particularly in the forex and commodity markets.

Example of Fundamental Analysis:

Suppose you are considering trading a currency pair, and you discover that the central bank of one of the countries has recently raised interest rates due to robust economic growth. Concurrently, the other country is experiencing political instability. A fundamental analyst might interpret these factors as a potential for the currency of the first country to appreciate relative to the second, leading to a long trading position.

Key Differences Between Technical and Fundamental Analysis:

1. **Data and Information:** Technical analysis relies on historical price and volume data, while fundamental analysis considers a broader range of economic, financial, and geopolitical information.

2. **Time Horizon:** Technical analysis is often associated with short to medium-term trading, focusing on price patterns and trends. Fundamental analysis is typically used for longer-term investment decisions.

3. **Objective:** Technical analysis aims to predict future price movements based on historical data and patterns, while fundamental analysis seeks to estimate an asset's intrinsic value based on economic and financial factors.

4. **Subjectivity:** Technical analysis can be more objective, as it relies on clear chart patterns and indicators. Fundamental analysis may involve subjective judgments about the significance of news events and data.

5. **Applicability:** Technical analysis is widely used in trading stocks, forex, and commodities. Fundamental analysis is particularly relevant for evaluating stocks, bonds, and macroeconomic trends.

Strengths and Weaknesses:

- **Technical Analysis Strengths:** Technical analysis is well-suited for short-term traders and provides clear entry and exit signals. It can be effective in identifying trends and momentum.

- **Technical Analysis Weaknesses:** It does not consider the underlying fundamentals of an asset, making it less effective for longer-term investors. It may also be less useful during periods of significant news-driven market volatility.

- **Fundamental Analysis Strengths:** Fundamental analysis is valuable for long-term investors seeking to understand the intrinsic value of assets. It can provide insights into the broader economic context.

- **Fundamental Analysis Weaknesses:** It may not provide precise entry and exit points, making it less suitable for short-term trading. Fundamental analysis may also be less effective during periods of market irrationality or speculation.

In conclusion, technical analysis and fundamental analysis are two distinct methods of analysis in trading, each with its strengths and weaknesses. Traders often choose one or a combination of both methods, depending on their trading style, objectives, and the assets they trade. Ultimately, the effectiveness of either approach depends on the trader's ability to interpret and apply the analysis effectively in their trading decisions.

Chapter 27

What Are Charts and Trends?

Charts and trends are fundamental aspects of technical analysis in trading. Traders use price charts to visualize historical price movements and identify patterns and trends that can help them make informed trading decisions. In this chapter, we will delve into the importance of charts and trends, how they are used in trading, and provide detailed explanations along with real-world examples.

Price Charts:

Price charts are graphical representations of historical price data for a particular financial asset, such as stocks, currencies, commodities, or cryptocurrencies. These charts display the asset's price over a specified time period, helping traders visualize how prices have evolved. The most common types of price charts include line charts, bar charts, and candlestick charts.

Key Aspects of Price Charts:

1. **Time Frame:** Traders can choose different time frames for their charts, such as daily, weekly, or intraday (e.g., 15-minute or 1-hour charts), depending on their trading style and objectives.

2. **Price Scale:** Charts can have either a linear or logarithmic price scale. Linear scales represent price movements proportionally, while logarithmic scales show percentage changes.

3. **Data Points:** Each data point on a chart typically represents the closing price of the asset at a specific time interval, depending on the selected time frame.

Types of Charts:

1. **Line Charts:** Line charts connect closing prices over time, creating a continuous line that provides a simplified view of price trends. They are useful for identifying long-term trends and basic support and resistance levels.

2. **Bar Charts:** Bar charts display a vertical bar for each time interval, with the top of the bar representing the high price, the bottom representing the low price, and a horizontal line indicating the opening and closing prices.

3. **Candlestick Charts:** Candlestick charts are similar to bar charts but provide more visual information. Each "candlestick" consists of a rectangular body, representing the price range between the opening and closing prices, and "wicks" (or "shadows") that extend above and below the body, showing the high and low prices.

Trends in Trading:

Trends are one of the core concepts in technical analysis and refer to the general direction in which an asset's price is moving over a specific time frame. Traders use trends to make predictions about future price movements and identify potential entry and exit points. There are three main types of trends:

1. **Uptrend:** An uptrend is characterized by higher highs and higher lows, indicating that the asset's price is generally rising. Traders often look for opportunities to buy or go long in an uptrend.

2. **Downtrend:** A downtrend is marked by lower highs and lower lows, signaling that the asset's price is generally falling. Traders may seek opportunities to sell or go short in a downtrend.

3. **Sideways or Range-Bound Trend:** In a sideways or range-bound trend, the price moves within a horizontal range, with neither significant upward nor downward momentum. Traders may employ range-trading strategies in such conditions.

Example of Charts and Trends in Trading:

Imagine you are analyzing the price chart of a popular cryptocurrency like Bitcoin (BTC) on a daily time frame. You notice that over the past several months, BTC has been consistently forming higher highs and higher lows. This pattern indicates a clear uptrend, suggesting that buyers have been dominant. As a trader, you may consider entering a long position or buying BTC in anticipation of further price appreciation.

In conclusion, price charts and trends are essential tools in technical analysis, enabling traders to visualize historical price data and identify patterns that can guide their trading decisions. By understanding chart types and recognizing different types of trends, traders can better assess market conditions, define entry and exit points, and develop trading strategies that align with their objectives and risk tolerance.

Chapter 28

What Are Chart Patterns?

Chart patterns play a significant role in technical analysis, providing traders with visual representations of historical price movements that can help predict future price directions. These patterns are formed by the collective behavior of market participants and are used to identify potential trend reversals or continuations. In this chapter, we will explore the importance of chart patterns in trading, the different types of patterns, and provide detailed explanations along with real-world examples.

Importance of Chart Patterns:

Chart patterns are essential tools for traders because they help interpret market sentiment, pinpoint potential entry and exit points, and manage risk. Recognizing these patterns can enhance a trader's ability to make informed decisions and increase the likelihood of profitable trades.

Types of Chart Patterns:

There are two main categories of chart patterns: reversal patterns and continuation patterns.

Reversal Patterns:

Reversal patterns signal a potential change in the prevailing trend direction. Traders use these patterns to anticipate trend reversals and adjust their positions accordingly. Common reversal patterns include:

1. **Head and Shoulders:** This pattern consists of three peaks, with the middle peak (the head) higher than the two surrounding peaks (the shoulders). A head and shoulders pattern indicates a potential shift from an uptrend to a downtrend or vice versa.

2. **Double Top and Double Bottom:** A double top pattern forms after an uptrend and suggests a potential trend reversal. Conversely, a double bottom pattern occurs after a downtrend and indicates a possible trend reversal to the upside.

Continuation Patterns:

Continuation patterns suggest that the prevailing trend is likely to continue after a brief consolidation or pause. Traders use these patterns to identify opportunities to enter trades in the direction of the existing trend. Common continuation patterns include:

1. **Flags and Pennants:** Flags are rectangular-shaped patterns that slope against the prevailing trend, while pennants are small symmetrical triangles. Both patterns indicate a temporary pause in the trend before it continues.

2. **Ascending and Descending Triangles:** Ascending triangles have a flat upper trendline and a rising lower trendline, while descending triangles have a flat lower trendline and a descending upper trendline. These patterns suggest a breakout in the direction of the prevailing trend.

Example of Chart Patterns in Trading:

Suppose you are analyzing a stock chart and identify a double bottom pattern forming after a prolonged downtrend. The first bottom forms, followed by a temporary bounce, and then the second bottom forms at a similar price level. This pattern may indicate that selling pressure is diminishing, and a potential trend reversal to the upside could be imminent. As a trader, you decide to enter a long position based on the double bottom pattern, with a stop-loss order in place to manage risk.

Key Considerations:

- **Confirmation:** It's essential to wait for confirmation before acting on a chart pattern. Confirmation may come in the form of a breakout or a specific price movement that validates the pattern.

- **False Signals:** Not all chart patterns lead to successful trades. Traders should be aware of the possibility of false signals and use risk management strategies to limit losses.

- **Timeframes:** Chart patterns can appear on various timeframes, from intraday charts to daily and weekly charts. Traders should select timeframes that align with their trading strategies and objectives.

In conclusion, chart patterns are powerful tools in technical analysis that provide traders with valuable insights into potential trend reversals or continuations. By understanding and correctly identifying these patterns, traders can enhance their decision-making process, manage risk effectively, and develop strategies that align with their trading goals.

Chapter 29

Technical Analysis Indicators

Technical analysis indicators are mathematical calculations and visual representations used by traders to gain insights into historical price data and make informed trading decisions. These indicators are applied to price charts to identify trends, momentum, overbought or oversold conditions, and potential buy or sell signals. In this chapter, we will explore the significance of technical analysis indicators, the different types of indicators, and provide detailed explanations along with real-world examples.

Significance of Technical Analysis Indicators:

Technical indicators serve as essential tools for traders because they help interpret price data objectively and provide quantitative measures of market conditions. Traders use indicators to:

- **Identify Trends:** Indicators help traders spot trends by smoothing out price fluctuations and providing a clearer view of the underlying market direction.

- **Confirm Price Movements:** Indicators can be used to confirm the strength and validity of price movements, assisting traders in distinguishing between genuine trends and noise.

- **Signal Potential Entry and Exit Points:** Many indicators generate buy or sell signals that traders can use as entry and exit points for their positions.

- **Highlight Overbought and Oversold Conditions:** Indicators like the Relative Strength Index (RSI) and Stochastic Oscillator can signal when an asset is overbought (potentially due for a price decline) or oversold (potentially due for a price increase).

Types of Technical Analysis Indicators:

Technical indicators can be categorized into several groups based on their functions. Here are some of the most commonly used types:

Trend Following Indicators: These indicators help traders identify and follow trends. Examples include Moving Averages, Moving Average Convergence Divergence (MACD), and Parabolic SAR.

Oscillators: Oscillators provide information about an asset's momentum and overbought or oversold conditions. Common oscillators include the Relative Strength Index (RSI), Stochastic Oscillator, and Commodity Channel Index (CCI).

Volume Indicators: These indicators analyze trading volume to confirm price movements and trends. On-Balance Volume (OBV) and Chaikin Money Flow are examples of volume indicators.

Volatility Indicators: Volatility indicators measure the level of price volatility in the market. Bollinger Bands and Average True Range (ATR) are commonly used volatility indicators.

Leading vs. Lagging Indicators:

Indicators can also be classified as leading or lagging indicators:

- **Leading Indicators:** These indicators attempt to predict future price movements. For example, the Moving Average Convergence Divergence (MACD) generates signals that may precede price changes.

- **Lagging Indicators:** Lagging indicators follow price movements and provide signals after a price change has occurred. Moving Averages are often considered lagging indicators because they reflect past price data.

Example of Technical Analysis Indicators in Trading:

Suppose you are analyzing the price chart of a stock, and you notice that the stock has been trading in a range for an extended period. To confirm potential buy and sell signals within this range, you decide to use the Relative Strength Index (RSI), an oscillator that measures the speed and change of price movements.

If the RSI shows a reading below 30, it suggests that the stock may be oversold, indicating a potential buying opportunity. Conversely, an RSI reading above 70 may signal that the stock is overbought, indicating a potential selling opportunity.

By incorporating the RSI into your analysis, you can make more informed decisions about when to enter and exit trades within the trading range.

Key Considerations:

- Traders should choose indicators that align with their trading strategies and objectives.

- Overloading charts with too many indicators can lead to confusion. It's essential to select a few relevant indicators and understand their signals thoroughly.

- Technical indicators are not foolproof and may generate false signals. Traders should use additional analysis and risk management techniques to minimize losses.

In conclusion, technical analysis indicators are invaluable tools that help traders analyze historical price data and make informed trading decisions. By understanding the various types of indicators, their functions, and how to interpret their signals, traders can enhance their ability to navigate the markets and develop effective trading strategies.

Chapter 30

Charting Tools and TradingView

Charting tools are essential components of a trader's arsenal, providing the means to visualize price data, analyze trends, and make informed trading decisions. TradingView is a popular and widely used online platform that offers advanced charting and analysis capabilities to traders and investors. In this chapter, we will explore the significance of charting tools, the features of TradingView, and provide detailed explanations along with real-world examples.

The Significance of Charting Tools:

Charting tools are fundamental to technical analysis, as they allow traders to transform raw price data into visual representations that are easier to interpret. Key aspects of charting tools include:

- **Visualizing Data:** Charts help traders visualize historical price movements, patterns, and trends, making it easier to identify potential trading opportunities.

- **Analyzing Trends:** Charting tools provide tools and indicators that aid in trend identification, such as moving averages, trendlines, and Fibonacci retracements.

- **Setting Entry and Exit Points:** Traders can use charting tools to set specific entry and exit points for their trades, helping them manage risk and maximize potential profits.

- **Customization:** Many charting tools offer customization options, allowing traders to tailor their charts to their preferences and trading strategies.

TradingView Overview:

TradingView is a web-based platform that has gained widespread popularity among traders and investors for its comprehensive charting capabilities and user-friendly interface. Key features of TradingView include:

1. **Advanced Charting:** TradingView offers an extensive range of chart types, timeframes, and drawing tools to suit various trading styles. Traders can customize their charts with technical indicators, oscillators, and other analysis tools.

2. **Social Networking:** The platform allows traders to share ideas, analyses, and charts with a community of like-minded individuals. Users can follow other traders, comment on posts, and engage in discussions.

3. **Customizable Alerts:** Traders can set custom alerts based on price levels, technical indicator signals, or drawing tool interactions. These alerts notify users of potential trading opportunities in real-time.

4. **Integration with Brokers:** TradingView offers integration with many popular brokers, allowing traders to execute orders directly from the platform without the need to switch to a separate trading terminal.

Example of TradingView in Action:

Imagine you are a forex trader interested in the EUR/USD currency pair. You open TradingView, select a daily chart for EUR/USD, and add a few technical indicators like the Relative Strength Index (RSI) and Moving Average Convergence Divergence (MACD). As you analyze the chart, you notice that the RSI is nearing an oversold condition, while the MACD is showing bullish divergence.

With this information, you set an alert on TradingView to notify you if the RSI crosses above a certain level and the MACD histogram turns positive. When your alert triggers, you access your broker directly from the TradingView platform to execute a long trade on EUR/USD, taking advantage of the potential bullish momentum.

Key Considerations:

- TradingView offers both free and premium subscription plans, with premium plans providing additional features and data.

- The platform's user-friendly interface makes it accessible to traders of all experience levels, from beginners to advanced professionals.

- Traders should ensure that their chosen broker is compatible with TradingView for seamless order execution.

In conclusion, charting tools are indispensable for traders, enabling them to analyze historical price data, identify trends, and make informed trading decisions. TradingView, with its comprehensive charting capabilities, social networking features, and integration with brokers, has become a preferred choice for traders looking to enhance their technical analysis and trading strategies. By harnessing the power of charting tools like TradingView, traders can gain a competitive edge in the dynamic world of financial markets.

Chapter 31

Candles, Candlestick Charts, and Line Charts

Candlesticks, candlestick charts, and line charts are fundamental tools used by traders to visualize and analyze price movements in financial markets. Each of these elements serves a unique purpose in technical analysis, providing insights into market dynamics and potential trading opportunities. In this chapter, we will explore the significance of candles, candlestick charts, and line charts, along with detailed explanations and real-world examples.

Candles in Trading:

Candles, often referred to as candlesticks, are individual data points that represent price action during a specific time interval, such as a minute, an hour, or a day. Each candle displays four crucial price levels: the open, close, high, and low. Understanding these price levels is essential for interpreting market sentiment and direction.

- **Open:** The opening price is the first price level at which a trade occurs during the given time interval. It is represented as the left side of the candle's body.

- **Close:** The closing price is the last price level at which a trade occurs during the time interval. It is represented as the right side of the candle's body.

- **High:** The high price is the highest level reached during the time interval, represented as the upper wick or shadow of the candle.

- **Low:** The low price is the lowest level reached during the time interval, represented as the lower wick or shadow of the candle

Candlestick Charts:

Candlestick charts are a visual representation of price movements using candlesticks. These charts provide traders with a more detailed view of market sentiment and price dynamics compared to traditional line charts. Candlestick charts are composed of individual candlesticks, each offering valuable information about the price action during a specific time period.

- **Bullish Candles:** Bullish candles, often depicted as green or white, indicate that the closing price is higher than the opening price. This suggests buying pressure and a potential upward movement.

- **Bearish Candles:** Bearish candles, often depicted as red or black, show that the closing price is lower than the opening price. This signifies selling pressure and a potential downward movement.

- **Candlestick Patterns:** Candlestick charts are renowned for their candlestick patterns, which consist of specific combinations of candles that provide insights into potential trend reversals or continuations. Examples of candlestick patterns include doji, hammer, engulfing, and shooting star.

Line Charts:

Line charts are a simpler form of charting in which the closing prices for each time interval are connected with a line. While line charts lack the detail provided by candlestick charts, they are useful for depicting overall trends and identifying key support and resistance levels.

- **Trendlines:** Traders often draw trendlines on line charts to connect successive lows or highs. These trendlines help identify the direction of the trend and potential reversal points.

Example of Candlestick Charts vs. Line Charts:

Suppose you are analyzing the price movement of a stock over a specific trading day. On a candlestick chart, you notice a series of green bullish candles, indicating a consistent uptrend throughout the day. This information helps you decide to enter a long position.

On a line chart, you observe a continuous ascending line, confirming the uptrend. However, the line chart lacks the detailed information about individual price levels that the candlestick chart provides.

Key Considerations:

- Candlestick charts are particularly effective for short-term trading and identifying potential reversal patterns.

- Line charts are useful for long-term trend analysis and simplifying price data for a quick overview.

- Understanding both candlestick and line charts is valuable for traders, as they provide complementary perspectives on price movements.

In conclusion, candles, candlestick charts, and line charts are essential tools for traders to interpret and analyze price movements in financial markets. Candlestick charts offer detailed insights into individual price intervals and patterns, while line charts provide a simplified view of trends and key support/resistance levels. Traders often use both types of charts to gain a comprehensive understanding of market dynamics and make informed trading decisions.

In trading and technical analysis, various types of charts are used to visualize price movements and patterns. Here is a list of common chart types used in trading:

1. **Line Chart:** A basic chart that connects closing prices with a line, providing a simple view of price trends over time.

2. **Candlestick Chart:** A popular chart type that displays price data using candlestick patterns, showing open, high, low, and close prices for a specific time period.

3. **Bar Chart:** Similar to a candlestick chart, but it uses vertical bars to represent price data, with the top of the bar indicating the high price and the bottom indicating the low price.

4. **OHLC Chart:** Stands for Open, High, Low, Close chart. It displays four key price points for each period, with lines connecting the open and close prices and horizontal lines for the high and low prices.

5. **Renko Chart:** A type of chart that filters out small price movements and focuses on significant price changes. It uses bricks to represent price movements, with each brick having a fixed size.

6. **Point and Figure Chart:** A chart that represents price movements with Xs and Os, where Xs indicate rising prices and Os indicate falling prices. It filters out small price fluctuations and focuses on trend changes.

7. **Heikin-Ashi Chart:** A candlestick chart variation that uses modified calculations to smooth out price data, providing a clearer view of trends and reversals.

8. **Kagi Chart:** A chart type that focuses on price reversals. It uses vertical lines to connect high and low prices, and the direction of the lines changes when a reversal occurs.

9. **Tick Chart:** A chart that displays price data based on the number of trades (ticks) rather than time intervals. It provides a detailed view of intraday price movements.

10. **Range Bar Chart:** A chart type that represents price movements based on a predefined price range, rather than time intervals. New bars are created when the price moves outside the specified range.

11. **Volume Profile Chart:** A chart that displays the volume traded at different price levels, helping traders identify significant support and resistance levels.

12. **EquiVolume Chart:** A chart that adjusts the width of bars based on trading volume, making it easier to identify areas of high or low trading activity.

13. **Three Line Break Chart:** A chart that uses colored lines to represent price movements. New lines are drawn when price movements exceed a predefined number of lines.

14. **P&F (Point and Figure) Chart:** Short for Point and Figure chart, this type of chart focuses on price movements and filters out time. It uses Xs and Os to indicate uptrends and downtrends, respectively.

15. **Candle Volume Chart:** Combines candlestick patterns with volume data to provide insights into both price and trading activity.

These are some of the commonly used chart types in trading. Traders often choose the chart type that best suits their trading style and preferences for analyzing price movements and patterns.

The **Marubozu** is a significant candlestick pattern that can provide valuable insights into price trends and potential reversals. Here's an explanation of the Marubozu candlestick pattern:

Marubozu Candlestick Pattern:

A Marubozu is a single candlestick pattern characterized by having little to no wicks or shadows, meaning the open or close of the candle is very close to the high or low of the period it represents. It typically indicates strong buying or selling pressure, depending on whether it is bullish or bearish.

There are two main types of Marubozu:

1. **Bullish Marubozu:** In a bullish Marubozu, the candle has no upper shadow (wick) or a very tiny upper shadow, and the open is near the low of the period, while the close is near the high. This pattern suggests strong buying pressure and a potential continuation of an uptrend.

2. **Bearish Marubozu:** In a bearish Marubozu, the candle has no lower shadow or a very tiny lower shadow, and the open is near the high of the period, while the close is near the low. This pattern indicates strong selling pressure and a potential continuation of a downtrend.

Interpreting Marubozu Patterns:

- A bullish Marubozu suggests that buyers have dominated the entire trading period, indicating a strong uptrend. Traders may view this as a potential entry point for long positions or a confirmation of an existing bullish trend.

- A bearish Marubozu suggests that sellers have controlled the entire trading period, indicating a strong downtrend. Traders may consider this as a potential entry point for short positions or a confirmation of an existing bearish trend.

- The absence of shadows in a Marubozu pattern suggests that there was little to no price retracement during the trading period, emphasizing the strength of the prevailing trend.

It's important to note that while Marubozu patterns can provide strong signals, they should not be used in isolation. Traders often use them in conjunction with other technical analysis tools, such as support and resistance levels, trendlines, and other candlestick patterns, to make more informed trading decisions.

As with any trading pattern or signal, it's essential to practice risk management and consider the overall context of the market before making trading decisions based on the Marubozu pattern.

DEFINITION OF DOJIS

Dojis are a type of candlestick pattern used in technical analysis to analyze and interpret price movements in financial markets, such as stocks, forex, commodities, and cryptocurrencies. They are characterized by their unique appearance, with the opening and closing prices of an asset's trading period being very close to each other, resulting in a small or nearly non-existent candle body. Doji patterns are marked by the presence of upper and lower wicks or shadows, which represent the price range during the trading period.

The primary significance of doji patterns is to indicate market indecision or a potential reversal in the prevailing price trend. The interpretation of a doji pattern depends on its context within the price chart and its relationship with preceding and subsequent candlesticks. Here are some key points about dojis:

1. **Market Indecision:** Dojis often suggest a period of uncertainty and indecision among traders, where neither buyers nor sellers have a clear advantage. This equilibrium can be a sign of potential market reversals.

2. **Reversal Signals:** Depending on the context, dojis can serve as potential reversal signals. For example, a doji that forms after a prolonged downtrend may indicate a potential bullish reversal, while a doji after a prolonged uptrend may suggest a bearish reversal.

3. **Continuation Patterns:** In some cases, dojis can also act as continuation patterns, signaling that the prevailing trend is likely to persist.

4. **Variations:** There are different variations of doji patterns, such as dragonfly dojis (bullish reversal), gravestone dojis (bearish reversal), long-legged dojis (high volatility and uncertainty), and more. Each variation has its own interpretation.

Traders use dojis, along with other technical indicators and analysis tools, to make informed decisions about buying or selling assets. It's important to

131

consider the broader market context and use dojis as part of a comprehensive trading strategy rather than relying solely on them for trading decisions.

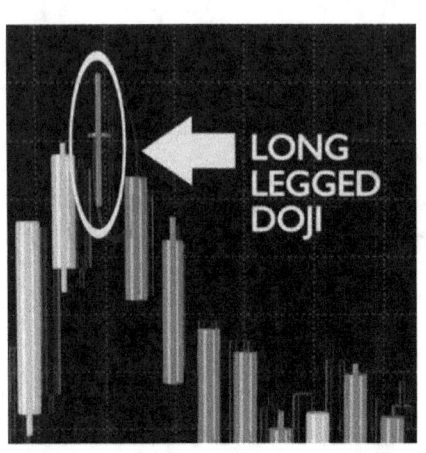

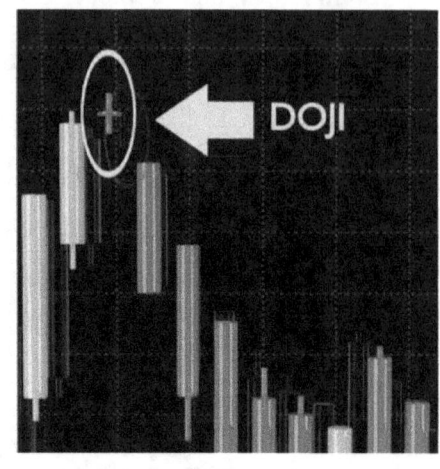

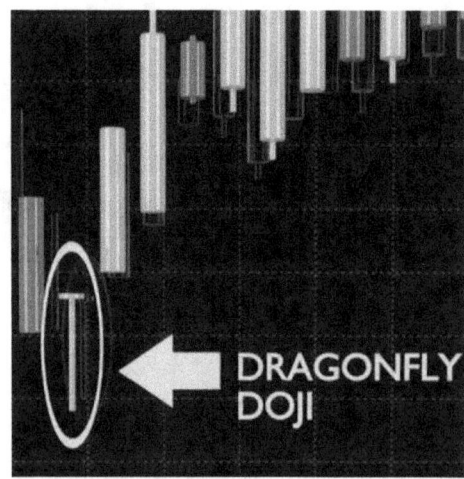

In trading, "dojis" are candlestick patterns used in technical analysis. They form when the opening and closing prices of a trading period are very close to each other, creating a small candle with both upper and lower wicks. Dojis often indicate a period of market uncertainty and can have different meanings depending on their context and placement on a price chart. Here are some common variations of dojis:

1. Classic Doji: In a classic doji, the candle has very close opening and closing prices, so the body of the candle is almost non-existent. This can indicate a period of indecision in the market, where buyers and sellers are in balance.

2. Morning Star Doji: This pattern forms after a downtrend. It begins with a large red candle, followed by a small doji, and then a green candle. This can suggest a potential reversal to the upside.

3. Evening Star Doji: This pattern forms after an uptrend. It starts with a large green candle, followed by a small doji, and then a red candle. This can suggest a potential reversal to the downside.

4. Dragonfly Doji: This doji has a long lower wick and an almost non-existent body. It can indicate that sellers attempted to push prices lower, but buyers managed to keep the price near its opening level, suggesting a bullish reversal.

5. Gravestone Doji: This doji has a long upper wick and an almost non-existent body. It can indicate that buyers tried to push prices higher, but sellers managed to bring the price near its opening level, suggesting a bearish reversal.

THERE ARE SEVERAL TYPES OF DOJI CANDLESTICK

1. Classic Doji: A classic doji occurs when the opening and closing prices are very close to each other, resulting in a small or nonexistent body. It signifies market indecision and can suggest a potential reversal or continuation depending on the preceding price action.

2. Long-Legged Doji: A long-legged doji has long upper and lower wicks, indicating significant price volatility during the trading session. It also reflects market indecision and can signal potential reversals or continuations.

3. Gravestone Doji: The gravestone doji has a long upper wick and a small or nonexistent body, suggesting that buyers initially pushed prices higher but were ultimately unable to maintain those levels. It can indicate a potential bearish reversal.

4. Dragonfly Doji: The dragonfly doji has a long lower wick and a small or nonexistent body, indicating that sellers initially pushed prices lower but failed to sustain the decline. It can signal a potential bullish reversal.

5. Four-Price Doji: In a four-price doji, the opening, closing, high, and low prices are all the same, resulting in a cross-like appearance. This pattern is relatively rare and signifies strong market indecision.

6. Rickshaw Man Doji: The rickshaw man doji has a small body with long upper and lower wicks, similar to a long-legged doji. It reflects uncertainty in the market and can precede significant price movements.

7. Hammers and Hanging Man Doji: These are variations of doji patterns. A hammer has a small body with a long lower wick and can signal a potential bullish reversal when it forms after a downtrend. Conversely, a hanging man doji has a small body with a long lower

wick and can signal a potential bearish reversal when it forms after an uptrend.

8. Morning Star and Evening Star Doji: These patterns consist of a doji or small-bodied candle followed by one or more candles in the opposite direction. The morning star doji appears after a downtrend and suggests a potential bullish reversal, while the evening star doji appears after an uptrend and suggests a potential bearish reversal.

These are some of the common doji candlestick patterns used by traders in technical analysis. Remember that while dojis can provide valuable insights into market sentiment, they should be used in conjunction with other technical indicators and analysis techniques for more reliable trading decisions.

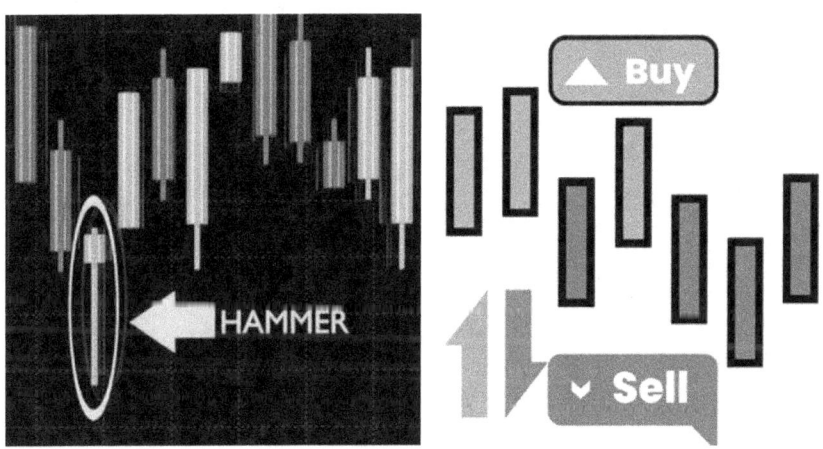

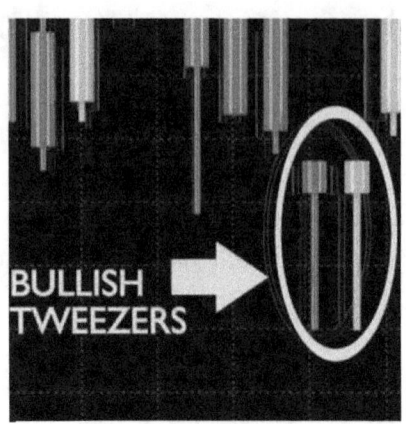

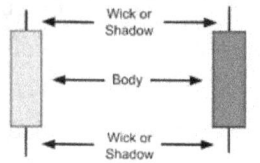

Idealized Japanese Candlestick

Wick or Shadow

Body

Wick or Shadow

Falling Three Methods

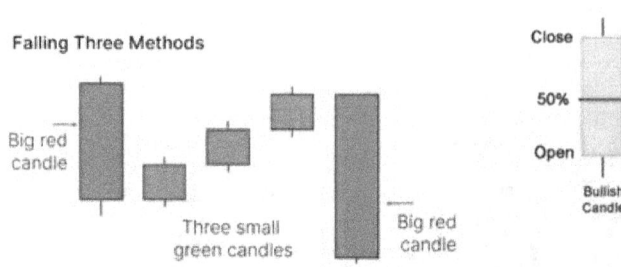

Big red candle

Three small green candles

Big red candle

Bearish Candle

Open

Close

50%

Open

Closed below 50% of the first candle

Close

Bullish Candle

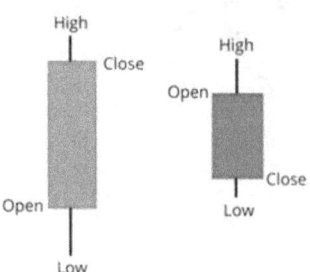

High

Close

Open

Low

High

Open

Close

Low

136

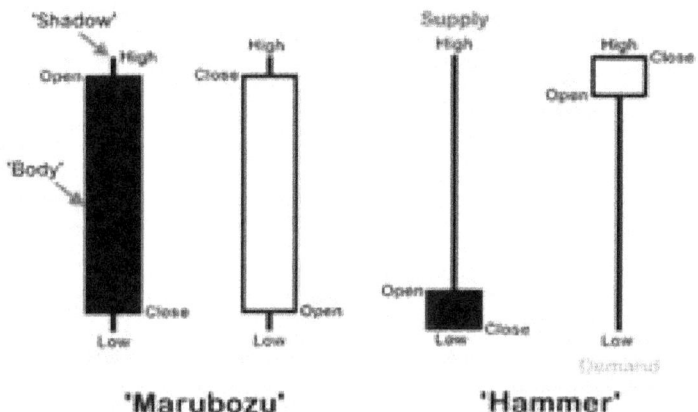

'Marubozu'   'Hammer'

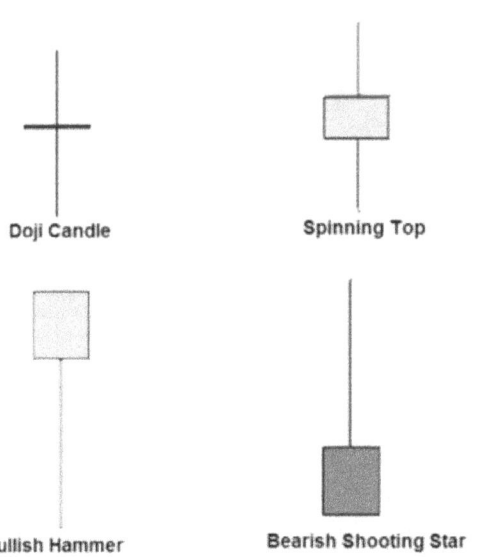

Doji Candle   Spinning Top

Bullish Hammer   Bearish Shooting Star

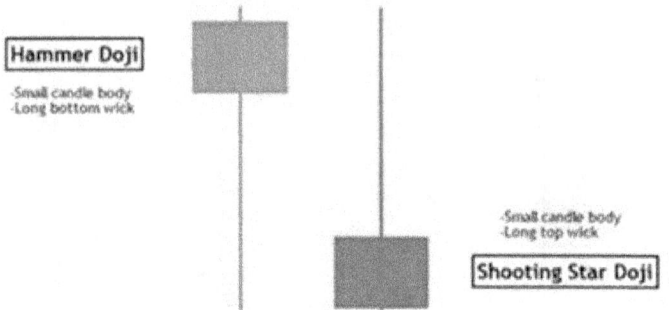

Hammer Doji

-Small candle body
-Long bottom wick

-Small candle body
-Long top wick

Shooting Star Doji

• **Bearish Evening Doji Star**

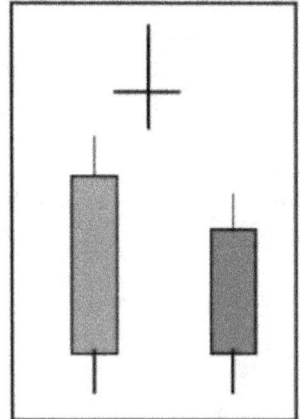

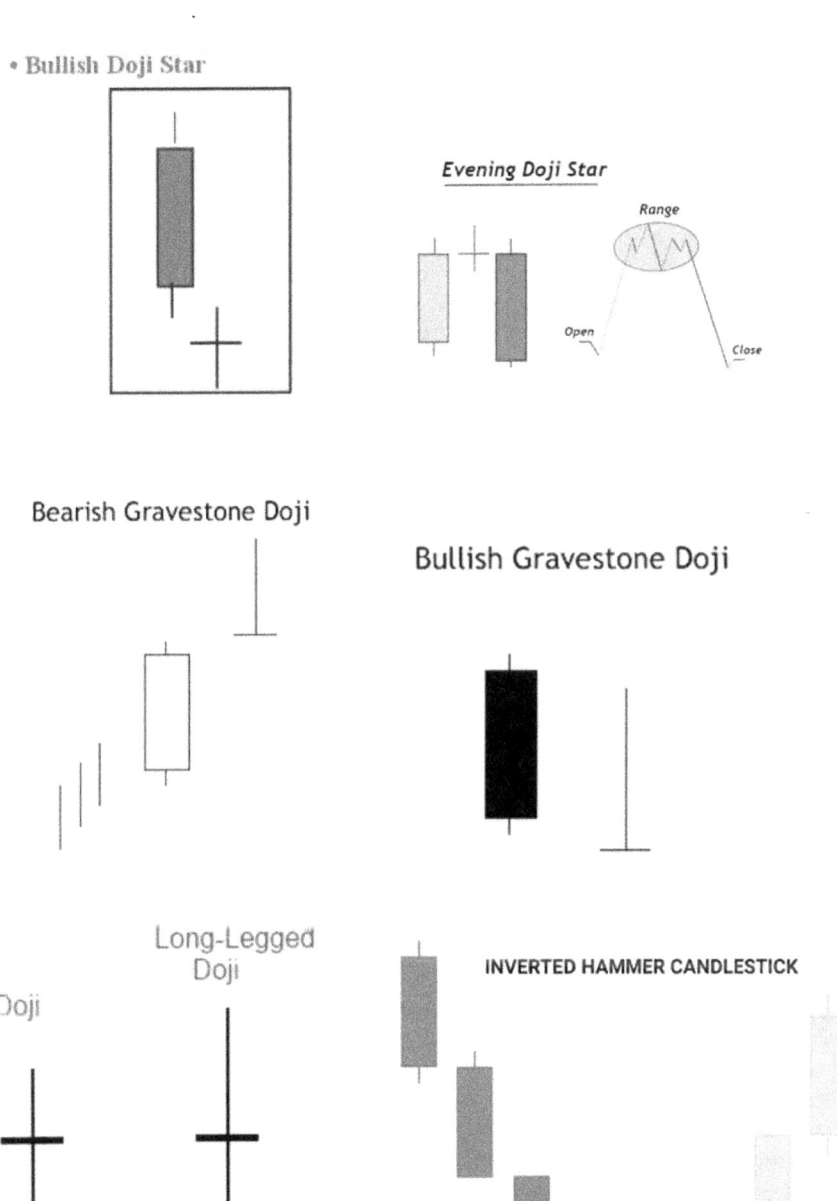

Bullish Doji Star

Evening Doji Star

Range

Open

Close

Bearish Gravestone Doji

Bullish Gravestone Doji

Long-Legged Doji

Doji

INVERTED HAMMER CANDLESTICK

Inverted Hammer Candlestick Pattern

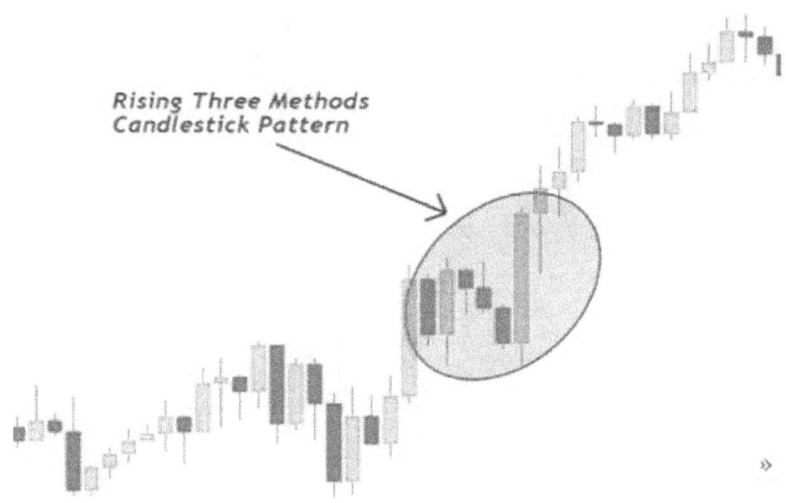

Rising Three Methods
Candlestick Pattern

Falling Three Methods

Bullish Morning Star

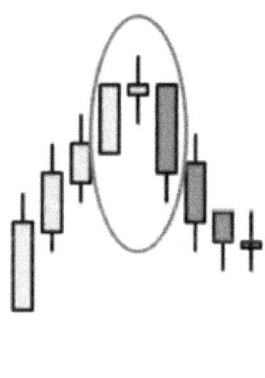

Bearish evening star

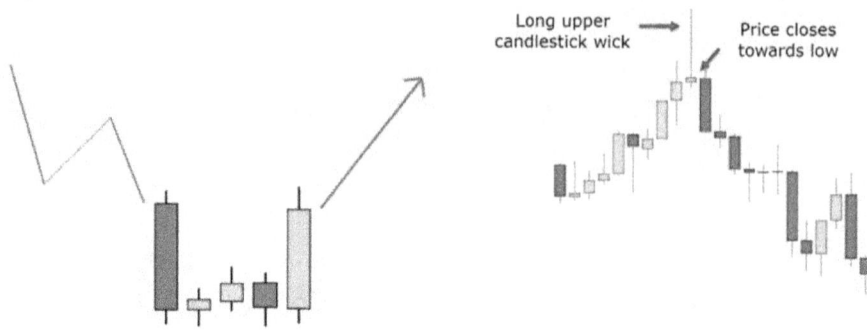

Tower Bottom Candlestick Pattern

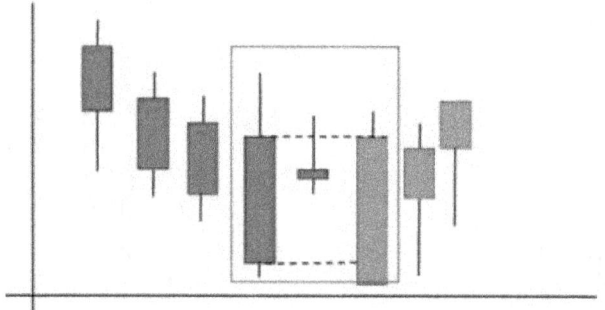

Variations in Bullish Engulfing Pattern

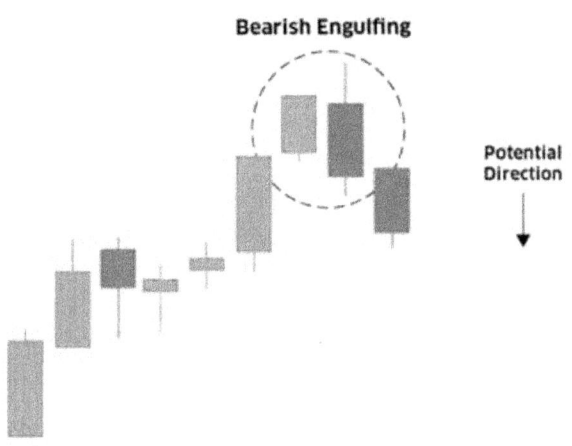

Bearish Engulfing

Potential Direction

Double top pattern

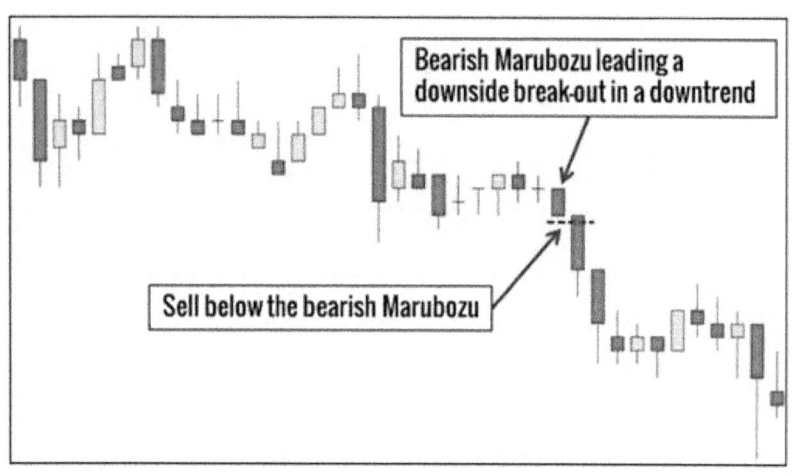

Bearish Marubozu leading a downside break-out in a downtrend

Sell below the bearish Marubozu

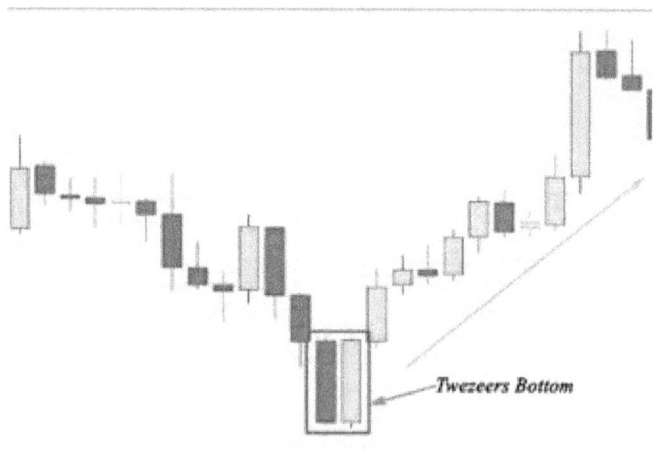

Twezeers Bottom

144

DEFINITION OF CONSOLIDATION IN TRADING

In trading, consolidation refers to a period when the price of a financial asset, such as a stock, currency pair, or commodity, moves within a relatively tight and narrow range after experiencing a significant price move. During a consolidation phase, the asset's price tends to exhibit reduced volatility and lacks a clear and sustained trend in either direction. This can be visualized on a price chart as a sideways or horizontal trading range.

Key characteristics of consolidation in trading include:

1. **Reduced Price Volatility:** Prices during consolidation tend to fluctuate within a defined range, and the amplitude of price swings is smaller compared to the preceding trend or market movement.

2. **Lack of a Clear Trend:** Consolidation is often seen as a "pause" or a period of indecision in the market, as traders and investors reassess their positions and await new information or catalysts.

3. **Sideways Price Movement:** On a price chart, consolidation typically appears as a horizontal or sideways pattern, with the asset's price bouncing between support and resistance levels.

Consolidation patterns can take various forms, including rectangles, flags, triangles, and channels, depending on the shape of the price range and how it is defined by support and resistance levels. Traders often use consolidation patterns to identify potential breakout or breakdown opportunities, where the asset's price exits the consolidation range and establishes a new trend.

Consolidation can be a challenging phase for traders, as it can lead to false signals and whipsaw movements, where prices briefly break out of the consolidation range but then quickly reverse. Therefore, traders often use technical analysis tools and indicators to confirm potential breakout or breakdown points and make informed trading decisions.

A LIST OF VARIOUS DOJI CANDLESTICK PATTERNS ALONG WITH A BRIEF DESCRIPTION OF EACH

1. Classic Doji: Small body with opening and closing prices close together, indicating market indecision.

2. Long-Legged Doji: Long upper and lower wicks, representing high volatility and indecision.

3. Gravestone Doji: Long upper wick, little or no body, suggesting potential bearish reversal.

4. Dragonfly Doji: Long lower wick, small or no body, indicating potential bullish reversal.

5. Four-Price Doji: All four prices (open, close, high, low) are identical, showing extreme market indecision.

6. Rickshaw Man Doji: Small body with long upper and lower wicks, signifying uncertainty and potential turning points.

7. Hammers: Small body with a long lower wick, signaling potential bullish reversal in a downtrend.

8. Hanging Man Doji: Small body with a long lower wick, indicating potential bearish reversal in an uptrend.

9. Morning Star Doji: A doji followed by a bullish candle and another doji, signaling a potential bullish reversal after a downtrend.

10. Evening Star Doji: A doji followed by a bearish candle and another doji, indicating a potential bearish reversal after an uptrend.

11. Bullish Doji Star: A doji that gaps below the preceding bearish candle, signaling a potential bullish reversal.

12. Bearish Doji Star: A doji that gaps above the preceding bullish candle, suggesting a potential bearish reversal.

146

13. Abandoned Baby Doji: A rare pattern involving a doji sandwiched between two gaps, signaling a potential reversal.

14. Tri-Star Doji: Three consecutive dojis with identical prices, indicating significant market indecision.

15. Tweezer Top Doji: Two dojis with matching highs, suggesting a potential bearish reversal.

16. Tweezer Bottom Doji: Two dojis with matching lows, signaling a potential bullish reversal.

17. High-Wave Doji: A doji with long upper and lower wicks, representing a state of confusion in the market.

18. Ladder Bottom Doji: A series of dojis with decreasing lows, suggesting potential bearish exhaustion.

19. Rickshaw Man Candlestick: A series of multiple dojis with small bodies and long wicks, indicating uncertainty and potential turning points.

20. Tri-Star Evening Star Doji: A combination of the tri-star and evening star patterns, signaling a potential bearish reversal.

21. Tri-Star Morning Star Doji: A combination of the tri-star and morning star patterns, indicating a potential bullish reversal.

Please note that some of these doji patterns are relatively rare and may not occur frequently in real-world trading. Traders often use doji patterns in combination with other technical analysis tools to make more informed trading decisions.

147

HERE'S A LIST OF VARIOUS DOJI CANDLESTICK PATTERNS

1. Classic Doji

2. Long-Legged Doji

3. Gravestone Doji

4. Dragonfly Doji

5. Four-Price Doji

6. Rickshaw Man Doji

7. Hammers (Bullish Hammer and Bearish Inverted Hammer)

8. Hanging Man Doji

9. Morning Star Doji

10. Evening Star Doji

11. Tri-Star Doji

12. Northern Doji

13. Southern Doji

14. High-Wave Candle

15. Ladder Bottom Doji

16. Mat Hold Doji

17. Inverted Mat Hold Doji

18. Meeting Lines Doji

19. Kicking Doji

149

40. Three Black Crows Doji

41. Three White Soldiers Doji

42. Three Stars In The South Doji

43. Three Stars In The North Doji

Please note that some of these patterns are relatively rare and may not appear as frequently as the more common doji patterns like the classic doji, long-legged doji, and others. Traders use these patterns to help identify potential reversals or continuations in price trends, but they should be used in conjunction with other technical analysis tools and indicators for more comprehensive decision-making in trading.

Chapter 32

What Are Trends and Trendlines?

Trends and trendlines are fundamental concepts in trading, helping traders identify the prevailing direction of price movements and potential reversal or continuation points. Understanding trends and how to draw trendlines is crucial for making informed trading decisions. In this chapter, we will delve into the significance of trends, the application of trendlines, and provide detailed explanations along with real-world examples.

Trends in Trading:

A trend in trading refers to the general direction in which the price of an asset is moving over a specific period. Recognizing trends is essential because they provide valuable insights into market sentiment and help traders determine whether to buy (in an uptrend) or sell (in a downtrend) an asset. Three primary types of trends exist:

1. **Uptrend:** An uptrend is characterized by a series of higher highs and higher lows, indicating that the asset's price is generally rising. Traders look for buying opportunities in uptrends.

2. **Downtrend:** A downtrend consists of lower highs and lower lows, signaling that the asset's price is generally falling. Traders seek selling opportunities in downtrends.

3. **Sideways or Range-Bound Trend:** In a sideways or range-bound trend, the price moves within a horizontal range, with neither significant upward nor downward momentum. Traders employ range-trading strategies in such conditions.

Importance of Trendlines:

Trendlines are diagonal lines drawn on a price chart to visually represent the trend's direction and slope. They help traders identify potential entry and exit points, as well as support and resistance levels within a trend. Trendlines are composed of two key components:

- **Support Trendlines:** Support trendlines are drawn beneath an uptrend, connecting the higher lows. They indicate price levels where buying interest tends to emerge and support the upward trend.

- **Resistance Trendlines:** Resistance trendlines are drawn above a downtrend, connecting the lower highs. They represent price levels where selling interest surfaces and resists further upward movement.

Drawing Trendlines:

To draw trendlines effectively, traders follow these general guidelines:

- Identify a clear trend by observing successive higher highs and higher lows (uptrend) or lower highs and lower lows (downtrend).

- Draw the trendline by connecting at least two significant points (lows for uptrends and highs for downtrends) with a straight line that does not intersect with price data.

- Extend the trendline to the right of the chart to identify potential future support or resistance levels.

Example of Trends and Trendlines in Trading:

Imagine you are analyzing the price chart of a popular stock. Over the past few months, you notice that the stock has been consistently forming higher highs and higher lows, indicating a clear uptrend. To confirm the trend's strength, you draw a support trendline connecting the successive higher lows.

As the stock's price approaches the support trendline, you identify it as a potential buying opportunity, expecting that buying interest is likely to emerge at this level, supporting the uptrend. This analysis helps you make an informed trading decision to enter a long position.

Key Considerations:

- Trendlines are subjective and depend on the trader's interpretation of price data.

- Traders should always consider using other technical indicators and risk management techniques in conjunction with trendlines to make well-informed decisions.

- Trends can change, and it's essential to monitor price action for signs of trend reversal.

In conclusion, trends and trendlines are essential components of technical analysis in trading, providing traders with valuable insights into market direction and potential entry/exit points. By understanding how to identify trends and draw trendlines accurately, traders can improve their ability to navigate the markets and develop effective trading strategies that align with their objectives and risk tolerance.

Chapter 33

Channels, Support, and Resistance

Channels, support, and resistance are critical concepts in technical analysis, helping traders identify potential price levels for making trading decisions. Channels, in particular, provide a framework for understanding price movements within defined boundaries. In this chapter, we will explore the significance of channels, how they incorporate support and resistance, and provide detailed explanations along with real-world examples.

Channels in Trading:

A trading channel is a price range within which an asset's price fluctuates over a specific period. Channels are defined by two parallel lines: an upper boundary, known as the resistance line, and a lower boundary, known as the support line. Channels can be classified into three main types:

1. **Uptrend Channel:** An uptrend channel is characterized by both the support and resistance lines sloping upward. Prices typically move higher within this channel, with the support line acting as a floor and the resistance line acting as a ceiling.

2. **Downtrend Channel:** A downtrend channel features both the support and resistance lines sloping downward. Prices tend to move lower within this channel, with the resistance line capping gains and the support line providing temporary relief.

3. **Sideways or Horizontal Channel:** A sideways channel, also known as a range-bound channel, occurs when the support and resistance lines are roughly parallel and horizontal. Prices oscillate within this channel, offering traders opportunities to buy near the support line and sell near the resistance line.

Support and Resistance within Channels:

Support and resistance are crucial components of trading channels:

- **Support:** The support line in a channel is a horizontal or diagonal line that represents a price level at which buying interest typically emerges. It acts as a floor, preventing prices from falling further within the channel. Traders often look for buying opportunities near the support line.

- **Resistance:** The resistance line is another horizontal or diagonal line that marks a price level at which selling pressure typically intensifies. It acts as a ceiling, hindering price advances within the channel. Traders often consider selling near the resistance line.

Example of Channels, Support, and Resistance in Trading:

Suppose you are analyzing a stock's price chart and notice that it has been trading within a clearly defined uptrend channel for several months. The support line in this channel consistently prevents significant price declines, while the resistance line limits further upward movement.

As the stock approaches the support line, you identify it as a potential buying opportunity because historical price data suggests that buyers tend to step in at this level. Conversely, when the stock approaches the resistance line, you may consider selling, as it indicates a point where selling pressure is likely to intensify.

By understanding the dynamics of the channel, support, and resistance, you can make informed trading decisions within this price range.

Key Considerations:

- Channels can occur on various timeframes, from intraday charts to daily and weekly charts.

- It's essential to confirm the validity of a channel by observing multiple price touches on both the support and resistance lines.

- Traders should use risk management strategies, such as stop-loss orders, to protect their positions when trading within channels.

In conclusion, channels, support, and resistance are essential elements of technical analysis that help traders identify price ranges and potential entry and exit points. By recognizing these patterns and understanding how support and resistance interact within channels, traders can improve their decision-making process and develop strategies that align with their trading goals and risk tolerance.

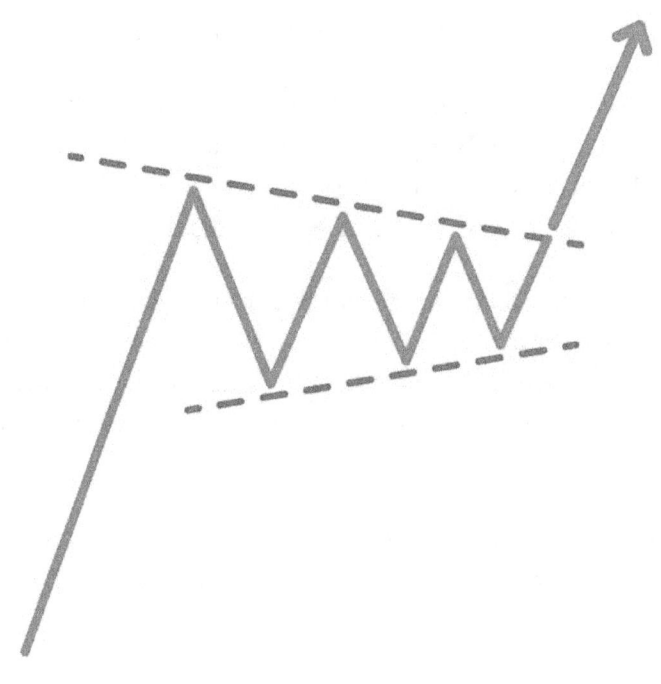

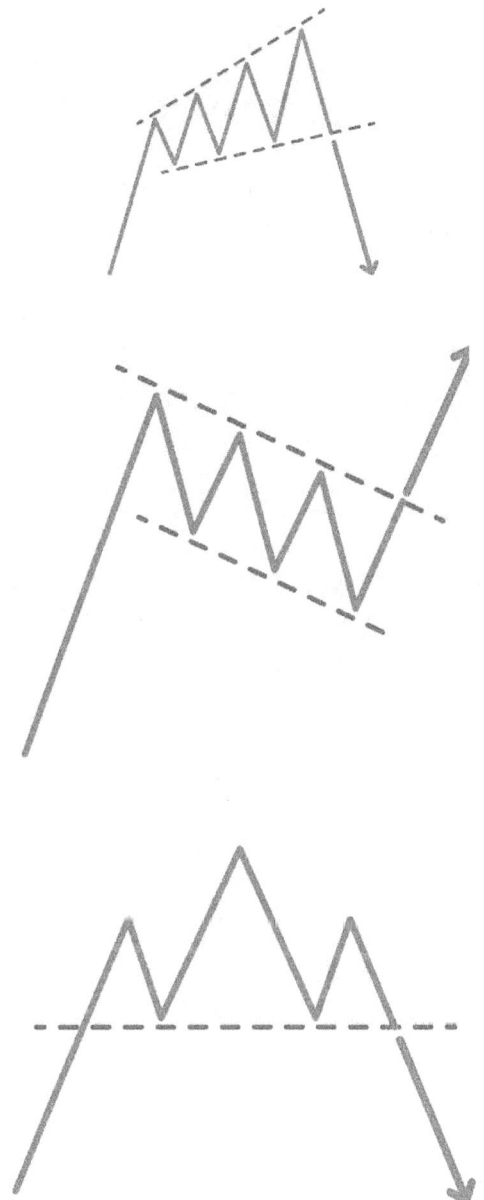

Chapter 34

What Is Volume?

Volume is a critical component of trading analysis, providing valuable insights into market dynamics and price movements. Understanding volume is essential for traders and investors because it can help confirm trends, identify potential reversals, and assess the overall strength of price movements. In this chapter, we will explore the significance of volume in trading, its various applications, and provide detailed explanations along with real-world examples.

The Significance of Volume in Trading:

Volume refers to the number of shares, contracts, or units of a financial asset traded during a specific time period. It is typically represented as a histogram or bar chart at the bottom of a price chart. Volume is essential in trading analysis for several reasons:

- **Confirmation of Price Movements:** High trading volume can confirm the validity of price movements. For example, a significant increase in volume during an uptrend suggests strong buying interest, reinforcing the bullish sentiment.

- **Identification of Reversal Points:** Volume can signal potential trend reversals. A sudden spike in volume accompanied by a sharp price reversal may indicate a shift in market sentiment.

- **Assessment of Market Strength:** Analyzing volume can help traders assess the strength of a price move. A price increase with high volume is often considered more robust than one with low volume.

Applications of Volume in Trading:

1. **Volume and Price Trends:** Volume can provide confirmation of price trends. In an uptrend, increasing volume as prices rise is

considered bullish. In a downtrend, rising volume as prices fall is seen as bearish.

2. **Volume and Reversal Patterns:** Traders often use volume to confirm or question the validity of reversal patterns. For example, a double bottom pattern followed by a surge in volume may be a more reliable signal of a trend reversal.

3. **Volume and Breakouts:** Volume can signal the strength of a breakout. A breakout from a trading range with high volume is often considered more significant than one with low volume.

Example of Volume in Trading:

Suppose you are analyzing the price chart of a stock that has been in a prolonged uptrend. As you examine the chart, you notice that the stock has recently experienced a significant increase in trading volume while continuing to make higher highs. This surge in volume reinforces your confidence in the ongoing uptrend, as it suggests strong buying interest supporting the price rally.

On the other hand, if you observe a price decline with a substantial increase in volume, it may signal a potential trend reversal. This scenario indicates that selling pressure has intensified, potentially leading to a shift in market sentiment.

Key Considerations:

- Volume analysis is often used in conjunction with other technical indicators and chart patterns to make informed trading decisions.

- Different markets (e.g., stocks, forex, commodities) may have varying average volume levels, so it's essential to consider relative volume changes.

- Volume data can be affected by news events, earnings reports, and other market catalysts, so traders should be aware of potential outliers.

Chapter 35

Understanding Fibonacci Retracement

Fibonacci retracement is a powerful and widely used technical analysis tool in trading that can help traders identify potential support and resistance levels on price charts. It's based on the Fibonacci sequence, a mathematical concept where each number is the sum of the two preceding ones (e.g., 0, 1, 1, 2, 3, 5, 8, 13, 21, and so on). When applied to trading, Fibonacci retracement levels are derived from these ratios and provide valuable insights into potential price reversals within a trend.

How Fibonacci Retracement Works:

To use Fibonacci retracement effectively, traders begin by identifying a significant price move on a chart, typically a recent swing high and swing low. These two points define the range within which the retracement levels will be applied. Once these points are determined, traders plot the Fibonacci retracement levels, which are typically set at key ratios, including 23.6%, 38.2%, 50%, 61.8%, and 78.6%. The 50% level, although not a Fibonacci ratio, is included due to its psychological significance.

Each of these retracement levels represents a potential area where price may experience a reversal or a pause in its current trend. The idea is that these levels can serve as support when the price is rising or as resistance when the price is falling.

Fibonacci Retracement Examples:

Let's explore a couple of examples to illustrate how Fibonacci retracement works:

160

Example 1: Uptrend

Suppose you are analyzing a stock that has been in an uptrend. You identify a recent swing low at $100 and a swing high at $150. Applying Fibonacci retracement levels to this range, you calculate the key levels as follows:

- 23.6% retracement level: $100 + (0.236 * ($150 - $100)) = $110.40

- 38.2% retracement level: $100 + (0.382 * ($150 - $100)) = $119.60

- 50% retracement level: $100 + (0.5 * ($150 - $100)) = $125.00

- 61.8% retracement level: $100 + (0.618 * ($150 - $100)) = $130.40

- 78.6% retracement level: $100 + (0.786 * ($150 - $100)) = $137.20

In this example, the trader would draw horizontal lines on the price chart at these Fibonacci retracement levels. These lines indicate potential support levels where the stock's price may reverse its downtrend and continue its upward movement.

Example 2: Downtrend

Now, let's consider a scenario where a currency pair is in a downtrend. You identity a swing high at $1.2000 and a swing low at $1.1500. Applying Fibonacci retracement levels, you calculate:

- 23.6% retracement level: $1.2000 - (0.236 * ($1.2000 - $1.1500)) = $1.1734

- 38.2% retracement level: $1.2000 - (0.382 * ($1.2000 - $1.1500)) = $1.1638

- 50% retracement level: $1.2000 - (0.5 * ($1.2000 - $1.1500)) = $1.1750

- 61.8% retracement level: $1.2000 - (0.618 * ($1.2000 - $1.1500)) = $1.1866

- 78.6% retracement level: $1.2000 - (0.786 * ($1.2000 - $1.1500)) = $1.1998

In this case, the trader would plot these Fibonacci retracement levels on the price chart as potential resistance levels, indicating areas where the currency pair may encounter selling pressure and reverse its current uptrend.

It's essential to remember that Fibonacci retracement levels are not guaranteed reversal points, and they should be used in conjunction with other technical analysis tools and confirmation signals to make informed trading decisions. Nevertheless, they can provide valuable guidance to traders by highlighting key price levels within a trend.

Fibonacci Retracement

UNDERSTANDING THE RELATIVE STRENGTH INDEX (RSI)

The Relative Strength Index (RSI) is a widely used momentum oscillator in trading that helps traders assess the strength and potential reversals in the price of an asset. Developed by J. Welles Wilder, the RSI is a versatile tool that provides valuable insights into overbought and oversold conditions in the market. In this chapter, we will delve into how the RSI works, its interpretation, and practical examples of its application.

How the RSI Works:

The RSI is calculated based on the average of an asset's recent price gains and losses over a specified period, often 14 periods. The formula for calculating the RSI is as follows:

$$RSI = 100 - (100 / (1 + RS))$$

Where:

- RS (Relative Strength) = Average of 'n' days' up closes / Average of 'n' days' down closes

The RSI value typically ranges between 0 and 100, with the following interpretations:

- RSI above 70: Indicates that the asset may be overbought, and there is a potential for a price reversal or correction.

- RSI below 30: Suggests that the asset may be oversold, and there is a potential for a price rebound or rally.

- RSI in the middle range (between 30 and 70): Indicates a neutral or ranging market without extreme overbought or oversold conditions.

Interpreting the RSI:

Traders use the RSI for various purposes, including trend identification, divergence spotting, and entry/exit signals. Here are some key ways traders interpret the RSI:

1. **Overbought and Oversold Conditions:** When the RSI crosses above 70, it suggests that the asset may be overbought, and a potential reversal or pullback may occur. Conversely, when the RSI falls below 30, it indicates oversold conditions, and a potential upward price movement may follow.

2. **Divergence:** Traders often look for divergence between the RSI and the price chart. Bullish divergence occurs when the RSI makes higher lows while the price makes lower lows, suggesting a potential reversal to the upside. Conversely, bearish divergence occurs when the RSI makes lower highs while the price makes higher highs, signaling a potential reversal to the downside.

Practical Examples:

Let's consider two practical examples to illustrate the application of the RSI:

Example 1: Overbought Conditions

Suppose you are analyzing a stock, and its RSI has recently crossed above 70, indicating overbought conditions. Simultaneously, the stock's price has been steadily rising. This could be a signal for traders to exercise caution and consider the possibility of a price correction or pullback.

Example 2: Bullish Divergence

In another scenario, you are monitoring a currency pair, and you notice that the RSI has been making higher lows while the price has been making lower lows. This bullish divergence suggests that the price might reverse to the upside. Traders might use this signal as a potential entry point for a long trade.

UNDERSTANDING BOLLINGER BANDS IN TRADING

Bollinger Bands are a popular and versatile technical analysis tool used by traders to analyze price volatility, identify potential price reversals, and determine price breakout points. Developed by John Bollinger in the early 1980s, Bollinger Bands consist of three key components: a middle band (typically a simple moving average), an upper band, and a lower band. In this chapter, we will explore how Bollinger Bands work, how to interpret them, and provide practical examples of their application.

How Bollinger Bands Work:

Bollinger Bands are primarily used to visualize price volatility. They are calculated based on a specified number of periods (typically 20) and a standard deviation factor (usually 2). The three components of Bollinger Bands are calculated as follows:

1. **Middle Band:** This is the middle line and is usually a simple moving average (SMA) of the asset's price over the chosen period. It represents the average price trend.

2. **Upper Band:** The upper Bollinger Band is calculated by adding two times the standard deviation of the asset's price over the same period to the middle band. It represents the upper volatility boundary.

3. **Lower Band:** The lower Bollinger Band is calculated by subtracting two times the standard deviation of the price from the middle band. It represents the lower volatility boundary.

Interpreting Bollinger Bands:

Traders use Bollinger Bands for various purposes, including identifying potential price reversal points and recognizing volatility patterns. Here are some key ways traders interpret Bollinger Bands:

1. **Volatility Assessment:** When the Bollinger Bands are narrow, it indicates low volatility, suggesting that the asset's price may be in a

166

period of consolidation or range-bound trading. Conversely, when the bands widen, it signals high volatility and the possibility of significant price movements.

2. **Overbought and Oversold Conditions:** When the price touches or crosses the upper Bollinger Band, it may indicate overbought conditions, suggesting a potential price correction or reversal to the downside. Conversely, when the price touches or crosses the lower Bollinger Band, it may signal oversold conditions and a potential price reversal to the upside.

Practical Examples:

Let's consider two practical examples to illustrate the application of Bollinger Bands:

Example 1: Volatility Squeeze

Suppose you are analyzing a stock, and you notice that its Bollinger Bands have been narrowing over the past several weeks, indicating decreasing volatility. This volatility squeeze suggests that the stock may be preparing for a significant price move. Traders often use this pattern to anticipate breakouts and consider entering trades when the price breaks out of the narrow range.

Example 2: Overbought Conditions

In another scenario, you are monitoring a cryptocurrency, and the price has recently touched or crossed the upper Bollinger Band. This may indicate overbought conditions, suggesting that a price correction or reversal to the downside may be imminent. Traders might use this signal as a potential exit point for a long trade or even consider shorting the asset.

In conclusion, Bollinger Bands are a valuable technical analysis tool that helps traders assess price volatility, identify potential overbought or oversold conditions, and anticipate price breakouts. They can be a useful addition to a trader's toolkit when used in conjunction with other analysis methods and risk management strategies.

Bollinger Bands Indicator

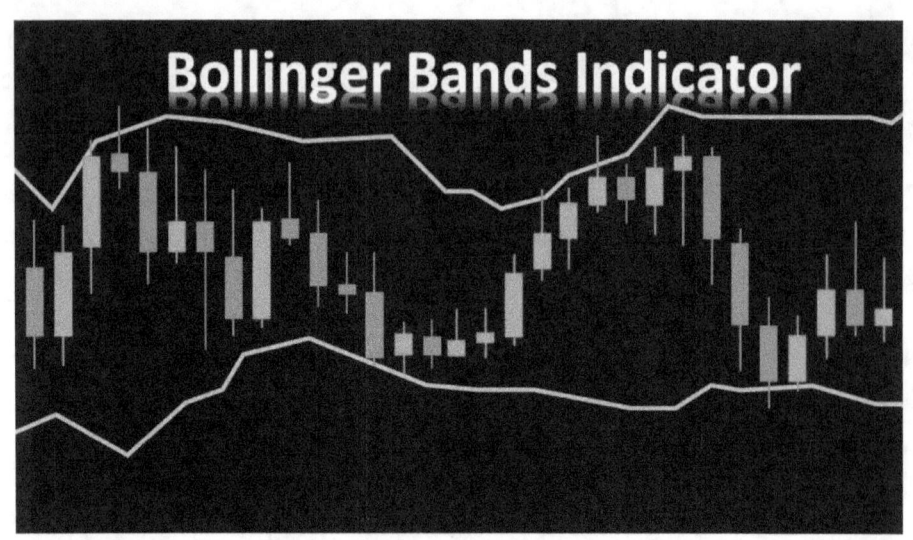

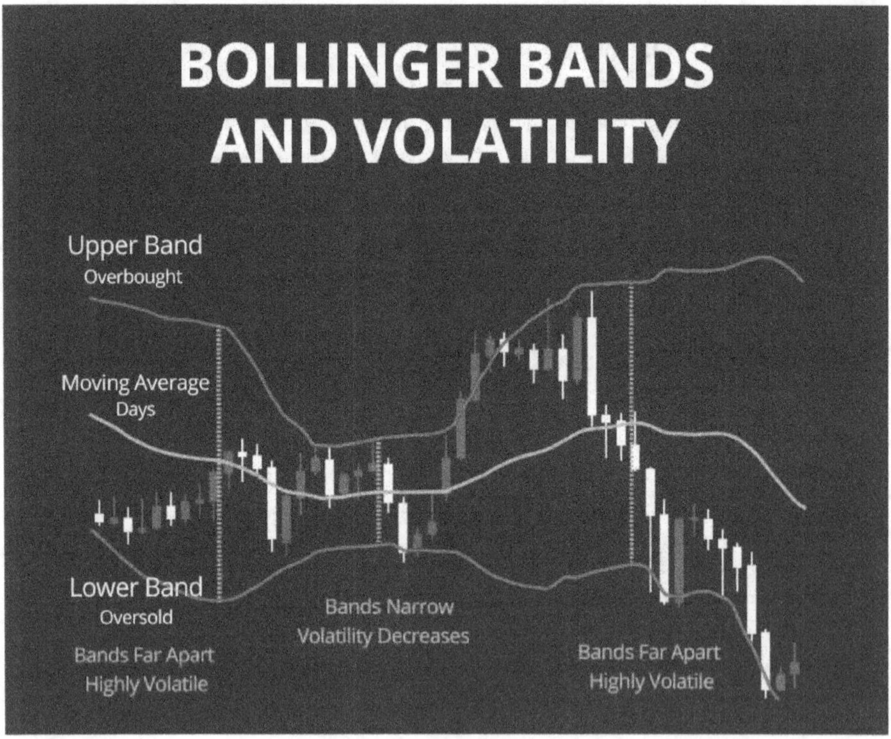

BOLLINGER BANDS
AND VOLATILITY
Upper Band
Overbought
Moving Average
Days
Lower Band
Oversold
Bands Far Apart
Highly Volatile
Bands Narrow
Volatility Decreases
Bands Far Apart
Highly Volatile

Chapter 36

Double / Multiple Tops and Bottoms

Double and multiple tops and bottoms are chart patterns that play a significant role in technical analysis, helping traders identify potential trend reversal points in the financial markets. These patterns are characterized by price levels where the asset's price has encountered resistance or support on multiple occasions. In this chapter, we will explore the significance of double and multiple tops and bottoms, provide detailed explanations, and illustrate their relevance through real-world examples.

Understanding Double/Multiple Tops and Bottoms:

Double tops and double bottoms are reversal patterns that occur after an extended trend, signaling a potential change in market sentiment. Multiple tops and bottoms extend this concept, indicating more than two price reversals at specific levels. Let's dive into each of these patterns:

1. Double Tops (Bearish Reversal):

A double top pattern forms after an uptrend and consists of the following elements:

- An initial price rally, creating a peak.

- A temporary decline (correction) from the peak.

- A subsequent rally that fails to exceed the previous peak, forming a second peak near the same price level.

The double top pattern suggests that buyers have failed to push prices higher, indicating a shift in sentiment from bullish to bearish. Traders often use the confirmation of a downward breakout from the pattern's neckline (the support level connecting the two bottoms) to initiate short positions or exit long positions.

169

2. Double Bottoms (Bullish Reversal):

Conversely, a double bottom pattern occurs after a downtrend and is characterized by:

- An initial price decline, resulting in a trough.

- A temporary rebound from the trough.

- A subsequent decline that fails to breach the previous trough, forming a second trough near the same price level.

The double bottom pattern suggests that sellers are losing control, and buyers are gaining momentum, indicating a potential shift from bearish to bullish sentiment. Traders often look for confirmation of an upward breakout from the pattern's neckline (the resistance level connecting the two tops) to enter long positions or exit short positions.

3. Multiple Tops and Bottoms:

Multiple tops and bottoms extend the concept of double patterns, indicating repeated price reversals at specific levels over time. These patterns can provide stronger signals of potential trend reversals due to the multiple instances of resistance or support.

Example of Double/Multiple Tops and Bottoms:

Suppose you are analyzing a daily chart of a stock that has been in a prolonged downtrend. You notice that the stock has formed a double bottom pattern, with the first trough occurring at $30 and the second trough at $31. After the second trough, the stock experiences an upward breakout from the pattern's neckline at $32.

This breakout suggests a potential bullish reversal, as buyers have successfully pushed the price above the resistance level. Traders who identified this double bottom pattern might consider entering long positions, anticipating an uptrend in the stock's price.

Key Considerations:

- Confirmation of a breakout from the neckline is crucial before considering trading decisions based on double or multiple tops and bottoms.

- These patterns are more reliable when combined with other technical analysis tools, such as trendlines, support/resistance levels, and oscillators.

- Keep in mind that not all double or multiple tops and bottoms lead to trend reversals; some may result in false signals.

In conclusion, double and multiple tops and bottoms are essential chart patterns in trading, offering valuable insights into potential trend reversals. Traders who can recognize and effectively use these patterns in their analysis can improve their ability to make informed trading decisions and capitalize on changes in market sentiment.

Double Bottom Pattern

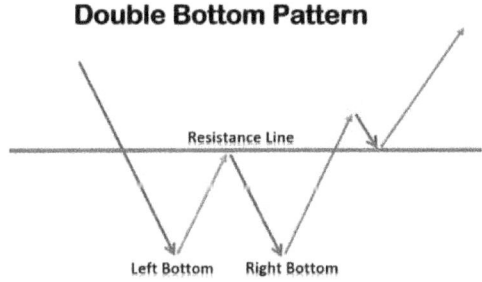

Double Top Pattern

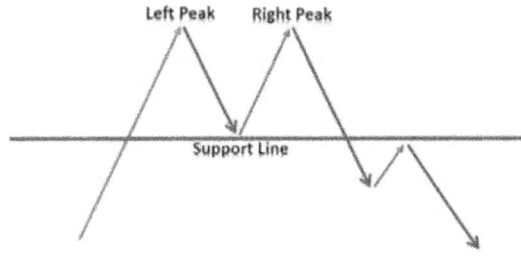

Chapter 37

Ascending and Descending Triangles

Ascending and descending triangles are chart patterns that traders use to identify potential breakout and trend continuation opportunities. These patterns are formed by connecting the highs and lows of price movements, resulting in distinctive triangular shapes on a price chart. In this chapter, we will explore the significance of ascending and descending triangles, provide detailed explanations, and illustrate their relevance through real-world examples.

Understanding Ascending and Descending Triangles:

Ascending and descending triangles are both continuation patterns, which means they often occur within existing trends and suggest that the trend is likely to persist after the pattern resolves. Let's delve into each of these patterns:

1. Ascending Triangle:

An ascending triangle is characterized by the following elements:

- A horizontal resistance line, which forms when the price repeatedly reaches a similar high.

- An ascending support line, which forms when the price consistently makes higher lows.

The ascending triangle pattern suggests that buying pressure is increasing, as reflected in the rising support line. However, sellers are still present near the resistance line. Traders anticipate a potential bullish breakout when the price decisively surpasses the resistance level, as it signals that buyers have overcome the selling pressure.

2. Descending Triangle:

Conversely, a descending triangle pattern consists of:

- A horizontal support line, created by the price consistently reaching a similar low.

- A descending resistance line, formed as the price continues to make lower highs.

The descending triangle pattern indicates that selling pressure is increasing, as evident in the declining resistance line. Buyers, however, remain active near the support line. Traders look for a potential bearish breakout when the price breaches the support level, suggesting that sellers have overwhelmed the buying interest.

Trading Strategies for Ascending and Descending Triangles:

Traders employ various strategies when encountering ascending and descending triangles:

- **Entry Strategies:** Traders often enter positions when the price breaks out of the pattern. For ascending triangles, this would be a long entry upon a bullish breakout, while for descending triangles, it would be a short entry following a bearish breakout.

- **Stop-Loss and Take-Profit Levels:** Traders typically set stop-loss orders just below the support line (for long positions) or just above the resistance line (for short positions) to manage risk. Take-profit levels are often set at a distance equal to the height of the triangle pattern, projected from the breakout point.

Example of Ascending and Descending Triangles in Trading:

Suppose you are analyzing a daily chart of a currency pair in a prolonged uptrend. As you study the chart, you notice an ascending triangle pattern forming. The resistance line is horizontal at $1.20, while the ascending support line is at higher lows.

A bullish breakout occurs when the price surpasses the resistance level at $1.20, signaling that buyers have gained the upper hand. Traders who recognized this ascending triangle might consider entering long positions, expecting the uptrend to continue.

Key Considerations:

- Confirmation of a breakout is essential before initiating a trade based on ascending or descending triangles.

- These patterns are more reliable when complemented with other technical analysis tools and indicators to confirm the breakout direction.

- False breakouts can occur, so traders should exercise caution and use appropriate risk management strategies.

In conclusion, ascending and descending triangles are valuable chart patterns that provide traders with opportunities to identify potential trend continuation points. By understanding these patterns and effectively incorporating them into their trading strategies, traders can enhance their ability to make informed decisions and profit from market movements.

Symmetrical Triangle   Ascending Triangle   Descending Triangle

Chapter 38

Symmetrical Triangles

Symmetrical triangles are versatile chart patterns used by traders to identify potential breakout opportunities in the financial markets. These patterns are characterized by converging trendlines, creating a triangular shape on a price chart. In this chapter, we will explore the significance of symmetrical triangles, provide detailed explanations, and illustrate their relevance through real-world examples.

Understanding Symmetrical Triangles:

Symmetrical triangles are continuation patterns, implying that they often occur within existing trends and suggest a potential continuation of that trend once the pattern resolves. Let's break down the components of a symmetrical triangle:

- **Converging Trendlines:** Symmetrical triangles feature two trendlines, one ascending and one descending, that converge toward each other. The slope of these trendlines is approximately equal, forming a symmetrical or triangular shape.

- **Lower Highs and Higher Lows:** Within the triangle, the price alternates between forming lower highs (touching the descending trendline) and higher lows (touching the ascending trendline).

The symmetrical triangle pattern suggests that neither buyers nor sellers have gained a decisive advantage, leading to a period of consolidation and indecision. Traders anticipate a potential breakout from the pattern, which can lead to a significant price move in either direction.

Trading Strategies for Symmetrical Triangles:

Traders employ several strategies when dealing with symmetrical triangles:

175

- **Breakout Trading:** This strategy involves entering a trade once the price breaks out of the symmetrical triangle. A bullish breakout occurs when the price moves above the upper trendline, while a bearish breakout happens when the price moves below the lower trendline.

- **Entry Points and Stop-Loss:** Traders often enter positions near the breakout point, with stop-loss orders placed just outside the opposite side of the triangle. This helps manage risk in case of a false breakout.

- **Take-Profit Levels:** Take-profit levels are typically set based on the height of the symmetrical triangle pattern. Traders project this height from the breakout point in the direction of the breakout to estimate potential price targets.

Example of a Symmetrical Triangle in Trading:

Suppose you are analyzing a daily chart of a popular stock that has been trading in a sideways range for several weeks. As you study the chart, you identify a symmetrical triangle forming, with converging trendlines. The price has been forming lower highs and higher lows within the pattern.

A bullish breakout occurs when the stock's price surpasses the upper trendline, indicating potential buying pressure. Recognizing this symmetrical triangle, traders might consider entering long positions, expecting a breakout to the upside and a potential continuation of the previous trend.

Key Considerations:

- Confirmation of a breakout is crucial before initiating a trade based on a symmetrical triangle.

- Traders should be aware of potential false breakouts, where the price briefly moves beyond a trendline before returning to the pattern.

- Symmetrical triangles can vary in duration, with longer patterns potentially leading to more significant price moves upon breakout.

Symmetrical Triangle Chart Pattern

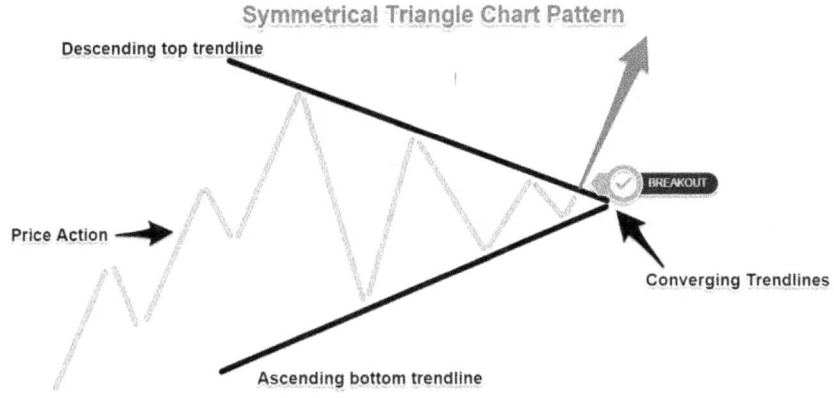

Descending top trendline

Price Action →

BREAKOUT

Converging Trendlines

Ascending bottom trendline

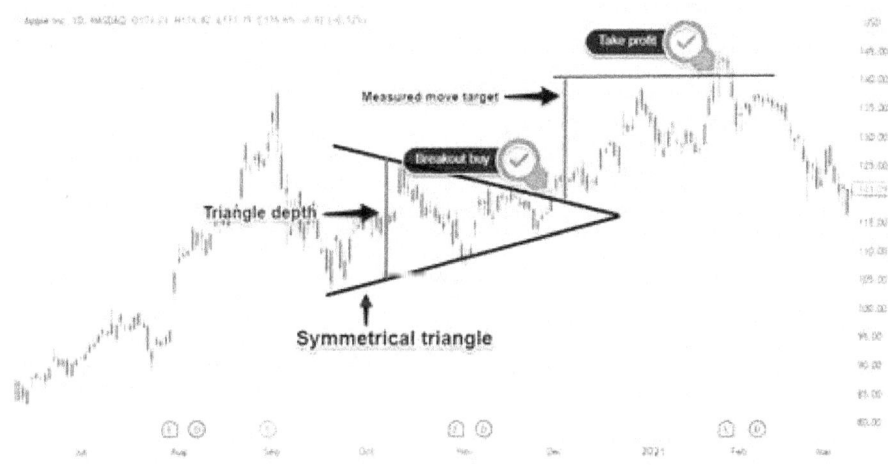

Measured move target →

Take profit

Breakout buy

Triangle depth →

Symmetrical triangle

Chapter 39

What Are Wedges?

Wedges are distinctive chart patterns that traders use to identify potential trend reversal or continuation opportunities in the financial markets. These patterns are characterized by converging trendlines that form a wedge-like shape on a price chart. In this chapter, we will explore the significance of wedges, provide detailed explanations of their various types, and illustrate their relevance through real-world examples.

Understanding Wedges:

Wedges are versatile patterns that can indicate either trend continuation or trend reversal, depending on their structure and the prevailing market conditions. These patterns have two primary forms:

1. **Rising Wedge (Bearish Reversal):** A rising wedge pattern features two converging trendlines. The lower trendline is steeper and has a more significant slope than the upper trendline. This pattern suggests a potential bearish reversal.

2. **Falling Wedge (Bullish Reversal):** A falling wedge pattern also consists of two converging trendlines, but in this case, the upper trendline is steeper and has a more significant slope than the lower trendline. The falling wedge pattern indicates a potential bullish reversal.

Rising Wedge (Bearish Reversal):

- **Lower Trendline (Support):** The lower trendline is drawn by connecting at least two significant lows in a manner that slopes more steeply than the upper trendline.

- **Upper Trendline (Resistance):** The upper trendline is drawn by connecting at least two significant highs and typically slopes at a gentler angle compared to the lower trendline.

The rising wedge pattern suggests that buying pressure is weakening, as indicated by the narrowing range between higher highs and higher lows. Traders anticipate a potential bearish breakout when the price decisively falls below the lower trendline, signaling a shift from bullish to bearish sentiment.

Falling Wedge (Bullish Reversal):

- **Lower Trendline (Support):** The lower trendline is drawn by connecting at least two significant lows and typically slopes at a gentler angle than the upper trendline.

- **Upper Trendline (Resistance):** The upper trendline is formed by connecting at least two significant highs and slopes more steeply than the lower trendline.

The falling wedge pattern suggests that selling pressure is diminishing, as evidenced by the decreasing range between lower highs and lower lows. Traders look for a potential bullish breakout when the price rises above the upper trendline, signaling a shift from bearish to bullish sentiment.

Trading Strategies for Wedges:

Traders employ various strategies when dealing with wedge patterns:

- **Breakout Trading:** Traders often enter positions once the price breaks out of the wedge pattern. For rising wedges, this would be a short entry following a bearish breakout, while for falling wedges, it would be a long entry upon a bullish breakout.

- **Entry Points and Stop-Loss:** Traders typically enter positions near the breakout point, with stop-loss orders placed just outside the opposite side of the wedge. This helps manage risk in case of a false breakout.

- **Take-Profit Levels:** Take-profit levels are often set based on the height of the wedge pattern. Traders project this height from the breakout point in the direction of the breakout to estimate potential price targets.

Example of Wedges in Trading:

Suppose you are analyzing a daily chart of a cryptocurrency that has been experiencing a strong downtrend. As you study the chart, you notice a falling wedge pattern forming, with converging trendlines. The upper trendline is steeper than the lower trendline, indicating a potential bullish reversal.

A bullish breakout occurs when the cryptocurrency's price surpasses the upper trendline, signaling potential buying interest. Recognizing this falling wedge, traders might consider entering long positions, expecting a breakout to the upside and a potential reversal of the previous downtrend.

Key Considerations:

- Confirmation of a breakout is essential before initiating a trade based on a wedge pattern.

- Traders should be aware of potential false breakouts, where the price briefly moves beyond a trendline before returning to the pattern.

- Wedge patterns can vary in duration, with longer patterns potentially leading to more significant price moves upon breakout.

In conclusion, wedges are important chart patterns that traders can use to identify potential trend reversal or continuation opportunities. By understanding these patterns and incorporating them into their trading

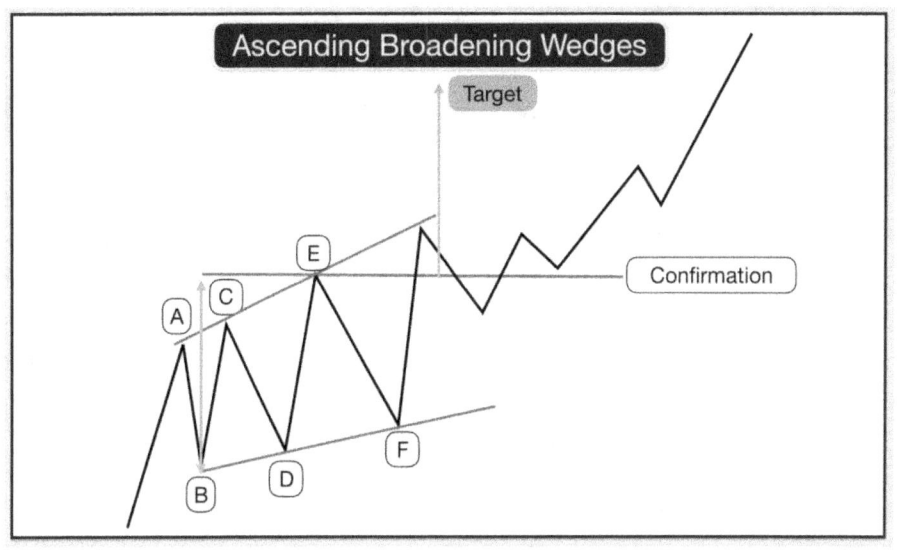

Wedge Pattern

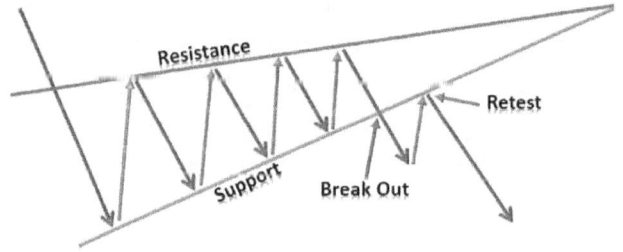

Chapter 40

Fundamental Analysis

Fundamental analysis is a crucial component of trading that focuses on evaluating the intrinsic value of financial assets by analyzing economic, financial, and qualitative factors. This analysis provides traders with insights into the potential future performance of assets, helping them make informed investment decisions. In this chapter, we will delve into the world of fundamental analysis, explore its key components, and provide detailed explanations along with real-world examples.

Understanding Fundamental Analysis:

Fundamental analysis aims to determine the true or intrinsic value of an asset, such as stocks, currencies, or commodities, by examining various factors that can influence its price. This analysis relies on the belief that an asset's price will ultimately align with its underlying fundamentals.

Key Components of Fundamental Analysis:

1. **Economic Indicators:** Economic indicators, including GDP growth, unemployment rates, inflation, and consumer confidence, provide insights into a country's economic health. Traders use these indicators to assess the overall economic environment, which can impact asset prices.

Example: If a country's GDP growth rate exceeds expectations, it may lead to increased demand for its currency, affecting exchange rates in the forex market.

2. **Corporate Financials:** For stocks and equities, analyzing a company's financial statements, such as income statements, balance sheets, and cash flow statements, helps assess its financial health and performance. Key metrics include revenue, earnings per share (EPS), and profit margins.

182

Example: If a company reports strong revenue growth and increasing profits, it may attract investors, potentially leading to a rise in its stock price.

3. **Interest Rates:** Central banks' decisions on interest rates can have a profound impact on financial markets. Changes in interest rates influence borrowing costs, investment decisions, and currency valuations.

Example: When a central bank raises interest rates, it can lead to higher bond yields, potentially making bonds more attractive than stocks for investors.

4. **Geopolitical Events:** Political stability, international relations, and geopolitical developments can affect asset prices and market sentiment. Traders monitor geopolitical events for potential market disruptions.

Example: A sudden political crisis in an oil-producing region can lead to increased oil prices, impacting energy stocks and commodities.

5. **Market Sentiment:** Market sentiment reflects investors' perception of an asset's value and future prospects. It can be influenced by news, social media, and overall market trends.

Example: Positive news about a company's product launch can create a bullish sentiment among investors, driving up the company's stock price.

6. **Supply and Demand Dynamics:** Understanding the supply and demand factors for commodities, such as oil, gold, and agricultural products, is crucial for commodity traders. Factors like production levels, weather conditions, and geopolitical tensions can impact prices.

Example: Drought conditions affecting crop yields can lead to reduced supply and higher prices for agricultural commodities.

Trading Strategies Based on Fundamental Analysis:

Traders use fundamental analysis to develop various trading strategies:

- **Value Investing:** Value investors seek undervalued assets based on their analysis of fundamentals. They buy assets they believe are trading below their intrinsic value and hold them for the long term.

- **News Trading:** Traders who focus on short-term price movements use fundamental analysis to react quickly to news events and economic data releases that can cause market volatility.

- **Sector Rotation:** Some traders rotate their investments among different sectors or industries based on their assessment of economic conditions and sector-specific fundamentals.

Example of Fundamental Analysis in Trading:

Suppose you are a forex trader analyzing the EUR/USD currency pair. You observe that the European Central Bank (ECB) is considering raising interest rates due to strong economic growth in the Eurozone. Simultaneously, the U.S. Federal Reserve (Fed) is signaling a potential rate cut due to economic uncertainties in the United States.

Based on this fundamental analysis, you anticipate that the euro (EUR) may appreciate against the U.S. dollar (USD) in the near term. As a result, you decide to enter a long position in the EUR/USD pair, expecting it to rise.

Key Considerations:

- Fundamental analysis requires a deep understanding of economic and financial data, as well as the ability to interpret the potential impact on asset prices.

- It is essential to use a combination of fundamental analysis and technical analysis to make well-rounded trading decisions.

- Traders should be aware of potential risks, including unexpected events or changes in market sentiment that can deviate from fundamental expectations.

In conclusion, fundamental analysis is a critical tool in trading that helps traders assess the intrinsic value of assets and make informed investment decisions. By understanding and applying fundamental analysis principles, traders can navigate financial markets with greater confidence and potentially capitalize on long-term opportunities.

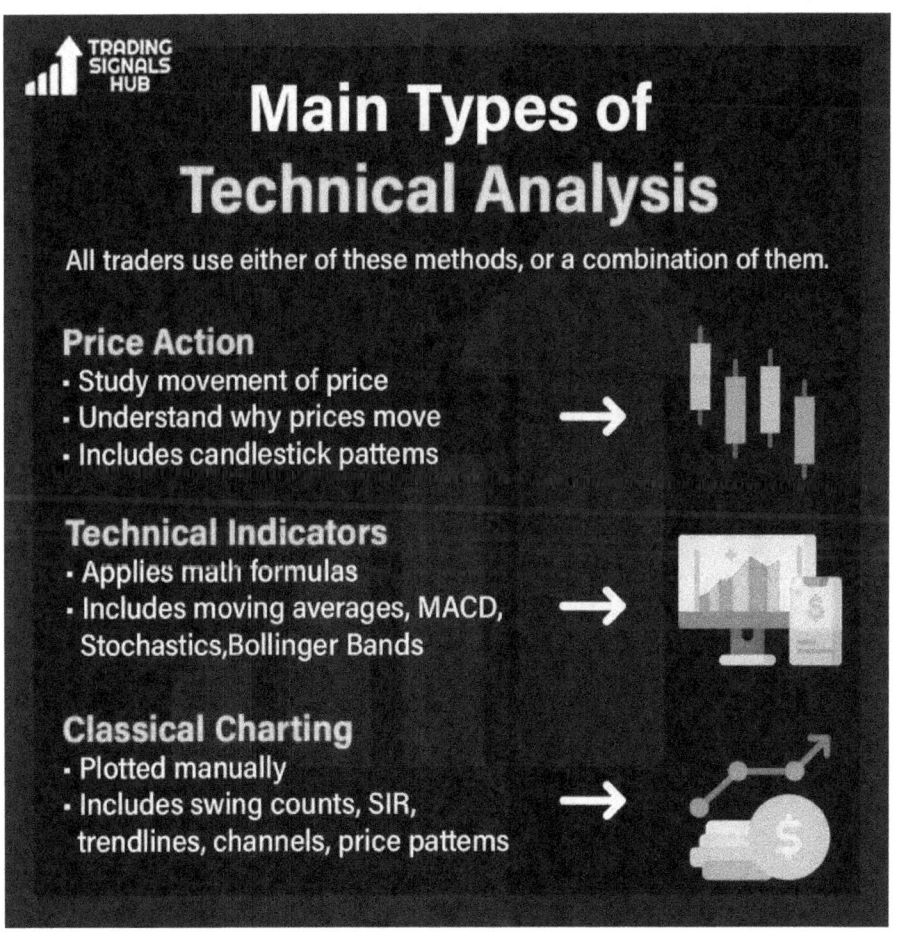

Chapter 41

What Is an Economic Calendar?

An economic calendar is a vital tool for traders and investors, providing a comprehensive schedule of upcoming economic events, announcements, and data releases that have the potential to impact financial markets. It serves as a critical resource for staying informed about scheduled economic indicators, central bank decisions, and geopolitical events that can significantly influence asset prices. In this chapter, we will explore the importance of an economic calendar, its key components, and how traders can use it effectively with detailed explanations and real-world examples.

Importance of an Economic Calendar:

An economic calendar is indispensable for traders and investors for several reasons:

1. **Scheduled Events:** It provides a schedule of important economic events, allowing traders to anticipate when key data releases or announcements will occur.

2. **Market Impact:** The calendar indicates the potential market impact of each event, helping traders assess its significance and the expected level of volatility.

3. **Risk Management:** Traders can use the calendar to plan their trading activities, including setting stop-loss and take-profit levels, to manage risk effectively.

Key Components of an Economic Calendar:

1. **Event Descriptions:** Economic calendars list various events, including economic data releases (e.g., GDP, employment reports), central bank meetings, corporate earnings announcements, and geopolitical events. Each event is accompanied by a brief description.

2. **Date and Time:** The calendar provides the date and time when each event is scheduled to occur. It is essential for traders to be aware of the time zone specified on the calendar.

3. **Previous and Expected Figures:** For economic data releases, the calendar typically displays the previous figure (the last reported data) and the expected figure (market consensus). This information helps traders gauge the potential market reaction.

4. **Actual Figure:** Once an event takes place, the economic calendar is updated to include the actual figure, providing traders with immediate information about the outcome and any deviations from expectations.

Using an Economic Calendar for Trading:

Traders can use an economic calendar as a valuable tool for making informed trading decisions:

1. **Planning Trades:** By knowing the timing of significant events, traders can plan their trades accordingly. For instance, a forex trader may decide to avoid entering positions just before a central bank interest rate decision.

2. **Volatility Assessment:** The expected impact of an event on the market is often indicated as high, medium, or low volatility. Traders can adjust their risk exposure based on this assessment.

3. **Event Strategy:** Some traders specialize in "event-driven" strategies, where they focus on trading around specific economic releases. For example, a trader might anticipate a bullish move in gold prices ahead of a weak employment report, as it could increase the likelihood of monetary policy easing.

Example of Using an Economic Calendar:

Suppose you are a stock trader with a portfolio that includes shares of Company XYZ. You regularly consult an economic calendar and notice that

Company XYZ is scheduled to release its quarterly earnings report after the market close today. The previous earnings report showed strong growth, and market analysts are expecting even better results this time.

Based on this information from the economic calendar, you decide to hold your position in Company XYZ, as you anticipate a positive earnings announcement that could lead to a rise in the stock price. You also set a stop-loss order in case the results deviate significantly from expectations to manage potential downside risk.

Key Considerations:

- It's important to stay updated with the latest information on the economic calendar, as events and data releases can be rescheduled or revised.

- Traders should combine information from the economic calendar with technical analysis and other market research to make well-informed trading decisions.

- Unexpected events, such as geopolitical developments or unforeseen economic data surprises, can still impact markets despite the information available on the calendar.

In conclusion, an economic calendar is an indispensable tool for traders and investors, providing valuable insights into scheduled economic events and their potential impact on financial markets. By utilizing this resource effectively, traders can enhance their ability to make informed trading decisions, manage risk, and capitalize on market opportunities.

13:30	CAD	▼ ▼	Building Permits (MoM)	7.4%	1.0%	4.1%
13:30	USD	▼ ▼	Initial Jobless Claims	298K	325K	321K
13:30	USD	▼ ▼	GDP Price Index (QoQ) P	2.0%	1.9%	1.9%
13:30	USD	▼ ▼ ▼	GDP (QoQ) P	3.6%	3.0%	2.8%
13:30	EUR	▼ ▼ ▼	ECB Press Conference			
13:30	USD	▼	Continuing Jobless Claims	2744K	2820K	2765K
13:30	USD	▼ ▼	Treasury Secretary Lew Speaks			
13:30	USD	▼ ▼	Real Consumer Spending	1.4%	1.5%	1.5%
13:30	USD	▼	Jobless Claims 4-Week Avg.	322K		333K
14:45	USD	▼	Bloomberg Consumer Confidence	-31.4		-33.7
15:00	USD	▼	Factory Orders (MoM)	-0.9%	-1.0%	1.8%
15:00	CAD	▼ ▼	Ivey PMI	53.7	59.0	62.8
15:00	VEF	▼	Venezuelan Retail Sales (YoY)	12.6%		14.5%
15:00	USD	▼	Factory orders ex transportation (MoM)	0.0%		-0.1%
15:30	USD	▼	Natural Gas Storage	-162B	-138B	-13B
17:15	USD	▼ ▼	FOMC Member Fisher Speaks			
22:30	AUD	▼	AIG Construction Index	55.2		54.4

189

Chapter 42

Risk Management

Risk management is a fundamental aspect of successful trading that aims to minimize potential losses while maximizing the potential for profit. Traders who prioritize risk management strategies are better equipped to navigate the volatile and unpredictable nature of financial markets. In this chapter, we will explore the importance of risk management, its key principles, and provide detailed explanations along with real-world examples.

The Importance of Risk Management:

Effective risk management is essential for several reasons:

1. **Preservation of Capital:** By controlling risk, traders can protect their trading capital from significant losses, ensuring that they have the resources to continue trading.

2. **Emotional Stability:** Risk management reduces the emotional stress associated with trading, as traders are less likely to make impulsive decisions driven by fear or greed.

3. **Consistency:** Consistent risk management allows traders to maintain a structured approach to trading, avoiding large drawdowns that can disrupt their trading strategies.

Key Principles of Risk Management:

1. **Position Sizing:** Determine the size of each trade or investment based on your risk tolerance and the potential loss. Position size is typically expressed as a percentage of your trading capital.

Example: If you have a $10,000 trading account and are willing to risk 2% per trade, your maximum risk per trade would be $200.

2. **Stop-Loss Orders:** Implement stop-loss orders to limit potential losses. A stop-loss is a predetermined price level at which a trade is automatically exited to prevent further losses.

Example: If you enter a long position in a stock at $50 and set a 10% stop-loss order, the trade would be automatically closed if the stock falls to $45, limiting your loss.

3. **Diversification:** Diversify your portfolio to spread risk across different assets or asset classes. This reduces the impact of a single investment's poor performance on your overall capital.

Example: Instead of investing all your capital in a single stock, you allocate it across various stocks, bonds, and commodities.

4. **Risk-Reward Ratio:** Assess the potential reward compared to the risk of each trade. A favorable risk-reward ratio ensures that potential gains outweigh potential losses.

Example: If you enter a trade with a 2:1 risk-reward ratio, you are risking $100 to potentially gain $200.

5. **Risk Tolerance:** Understand your personal risk tolerance, which varies from trader to trader. It reflects your ability and willingness to withstand losses without emotional distress.

Example: A risk-averse trader may opt for smaller position sizes and tighter stop-loss levels, while a risk-tolerant trader may accept larger risks for potentially higher returns.

Risk Management in Action:

Imagine you are a forex trader and decide to enter a long position in the EUR/USD currency pair at 1.1200. You have a trading account with a balance of $10,000, and you are willing to risk 2% of your capital on this trade. Therefore, you set a stop-loss order at 1.1150, which represents a potential loss of $100 (50 pips) if the trade goes against you.

With this risk management strategy in place, you have limited your potential loss to 2% of your trading capital, ensuring that even if the trade results in a loss, it won't significantly impact your overall capital. Additionally, you can calculate your risk-reward ratio by setting a take-profit order at 1.1300, potentially gaining $200 (100 pips) if the trade reaches your target.

Key Considerations:

- Risk management should be an integral part of your trading plan, and it is essential to stick to your predefined risk parameters.

- Avoid over-leveraging, which can lead to substantial losses. Leverage should be used cautiously and in line with your risk tolerance.

- Regularly review and adjust your risk management strategies as your trading capital, objectives, and market conditions change.

In conclusion, risk management is a cornerstone of successful trading. By following key principles such as position sizing, stop-loss orders, diversification, risk-reward ratios, and understanding your risk tolerance, traders can protect their capital and increase their chances of consistent profitability in the challenging world of financial markets.

Chapter 43

What Are Stop Losses?

Stop losses are a fundamental risk management tool used by traders to limit potential losses on their trades. They are pre-determined price levels at which a trade is automatically closed to prevent further losses. Understanding how to use stop losses effectively is crucial for protecting trading capital and minimizing the emotional stress associated with trading. In this chapter, we will delve into the concept of stop losses, their importance, different types, and provide detailed explanations along with real-world examples.

Importance of Stop Losses:

Stop losses serve several critical purposes in trading:

1. **Capital Preservation:** They help protect your trading capital by limiting the amount you can lose on a single trade. This ensures that a series of losing trades does not deplete your account.

2. **Emotional Control:** Stop losses reduce the emotional stress associated with trading. Knowing that a predefined level of risk is in place can prevent impulsive decisions driven by fear or greed.

3. **Consistency:** By implementing stop losses consistently, traders can maintain discipline in their trading strategies and avoid large drawdowns that can disrupt their overall approach.

Types of Stop Losses:

1. **Fixed Percentage Stop:** This is a common type of stop loss where traders set a specific percentage of their trading capital as the maximum acceptable loss for a trade. For example, if a trader has a $10,000 account and is willing to risk 2%, they would set a stop loss that limits the loss on the trade to $200.

2. **Trailing Stop:** A trailing stop is dynamic and adjusts as the price moves in the trader's favor. It allows traders to lock in profits while giving the trade room to breathe. If the price moves in the desired direction, the trailing stop automatically moves closer to the current market price.

3. **Volatility-based Stop:** Some traders use volatility-based stops that take into account the asset's historical price volatility. This type of stop adapts to market conditions and can be wider during periods of low volatility and tighter during high volatility.

Using Stop Losses Effectively:

1. **Setting Appropriate Levels:** Determine your stop loss level based on your risk tolerance and the asset's price volatility. It should be placed at a level where it provides protection but isn't too close to the entry point to avoid being prematurely triggered by minor price fluctuations.

2. **Adjusting for Market Conditions:** Market conditions can change, affecting volatility. Be prepared to adjust your stop loss levels accordingly to reflect changing market dynamics.

3. **Avoiding Arbitrary Decisions:** Never move or remove a stop loss order during a trade to avoid a loss due to emotions or hope for a reversal. Stick to your predetermined risk management plan.

Example of Stop Loss in Trading:

Imagine you are a stock trader and decide to enter a long position in Company ABC at $50 per share. You have conducted your analysis and determined that a reasonable stop loss level is $48 per share, representing a potential loss of $2 per share.

With this stop loss in place, if the stock price falls to $48, your trade is automatically closed, limiting your loss to $2 per share. This predefined risk level allows you to trade with confidence, knowing that your potential loss is controlled.

194

Key Considerations:

- Stop losses should be an integral part of your trading plan and should be set before entering a trade.

- Avoid placing stop losses at round numbers or common support/resistance levels, as these levels may be targeted by market participants.

- Traders should use stop losses consistently to maintain a disciplined approach to trading.

In conclusion, stop losses are a critical risk management tool in trading, helping traders protect their capital and maintain emotional control. Whether using fixed percentage, trailing, or volatility-based stops, traders can limit potential losses and improve their chances of long-term success in the financial markets.

Chapter 44

What Are Platforms?

Trading platforms, often referred to as trading software or trading terminals, are essential tools that enable traders and investors to access financial markets, execute trades, analyze data, and manage their trading accounts. These platforms come in various forms, catering to different asset classes and trading styles. In this chapter, we will explore the concept of trading platforms, their significance, key features, and provide detailed explanations along with real-world examples.

Significance of Trading Platforms:

Trading platforms serve as the primary interface between traders and the financial markets. Their significance lies in the following key functions:

1. **Market Access:** Trading platforms provide access to a wide range of financial markets, including stocks, commodities, forex, cryptocurrencies, and more. They connect traders to global exchanges and liquidity providers.

2. **Order Execution:** Traders can place, modify, or cancel orders directly through the platform. These orders are executed in real-time, ensuring efficient and accurate trade execution.

3. **Analysis and Research:** Most trading platforms offer comprehensive tools for technical and fundamental analysis. Traders can access charts, indicators, news feeds, and research resources to make informed decisions.

4. **Risk Management:** Platforms allow traders to set stop-loss and take-profit orders, implement trailing stops, and manage risk effectively.

Key Features of Trading Platforms:

1. **User Interface:** Trading platforms provide an intuitive and user-friendly interface that allows traders to navigate and execute trades efficiently. Charting tools, price quotes, and order entry windows are typically included.

2. **Asset Coverage:** Platforms differ in the range of assets they offer. Some focus on specific asset classes, such as stocks or forex, while others provide access to a wide variety of financial instruments.

3. **Order Types:** Platforms support various order types, including market orders, limit orders, stop orders, and more. These order types enable traders to implement different trading strategies.

4. **Technical Analysis Tools:** Robust charting capabilities, technical indicators, drawing tools, and customizable layouts are important features for traders who rely on technical analysis.

5. **Fundamental Analysis:** Some platforms provide access to fundamental data, news feeds, and economic calendars for traders who incorporate fundamental analysis into their strategies.

6. **Risk Management Tools:** Platforms allow traders to set stop losses and take profits, apply trailing stops, and calculate position sizes to manage risk effectively.

Examples of Trading Platforms:

1. **MetaTrader 4 (MT4):** MT4 is a widely used trading platform in the forex market, known for its comprehensive charting capabilities, automated trading (Expert Advisors), and extensive library of technical indicators.

2. **MetaTrader 5 (MT5):** MT5, developed by the same company as MT4, offers expanded features, including more timeframes, additional technical indicators, and access to a broader range of asset classes.

197

3. **Thinkorswim:** Thinkorswim, offered by TD Ameritrade, is a popular trading platform for stock and options traders. It provides advanced charting, analysis tools, and a customizable interface.

4. **Interactive Brokers Trader Workstation (TWS):** TWS is known for its global market access, extensive asset coverage, and advanced trading tools suitable for both retail and professional traders.

Choosing the Right Trading Platform:

Selecting the right trading platform is crucial, as it should align with your trading goals, preferred asset classes, and trading style. Consider factors such as usability, asset coverage, fees, research tools, and customer support when making your choice.

In conclusion, trading platforms are the central tools that enable traders and investors to access financial markets, execute trades, and manage their portfolios. Understanding the features and functionalities of different platforms and choosing the one that best suits your trading needs is essential for a successful trading experience.

Chapter 45

What Is MetaTrader 4 (MT4)?

MetaTrader 4, commonly known as MT4, is a widely used and highly regarded trading platform in the world of online trading. It was developed by MetaQuotes Software and has gained immense popularity among traders and brokers for its user-friendly interface, robust technical analysis tools, and extensive support for automated trading strategies. In this chapter, we will explore the features, functionalities, and significance of MetaTrader 4 (MT4) in the realm of trading, accompanied by detailed explanations and real-world examples.

Features and Functionalities of MetaTrader 4 (MT4):

1. **User-Friendly Interface:** MT4 offers a simple and intuitive interface that is accessible to traders of all levels, from beginners to experienced professionals. The platform's layout includes customizable chart windows, a market watchlist, and a trade execution panel.

2. **Charting and Technical Analysis:** MT4 provides advanced charting capabilities, offering a wide range of timeframes, chart types (candlestick, line, bar), and technical indicators. Traders can apply numerous built-in indicators or create custom ones to perform in-depth technical analysis.

Example: A forex trader using MT4 can apply the Moving Average and Relative Strength Index (RSI) indicators to analyze price trends and overbought/oversold conditions.

3. **Automated Trading:** One of MT4's standout features is its support for automated trading through Expert Advisors (EAs). Traders can create or download EAs, which are trading algorithms that execute trades automatically based on predefined criteria.

Example: A trader can develop an EA that enters a buy position when a specific combination of technical indicators signals an uptrend.

4. **Backtesting:** MT4 allows traders to backtest their trading strategies using historical price data. This feature enables traders to assess the performance of their strategies before deploying them in live markets.

Example: A stock trader can use backtesting in MT4 to evaluate the profitability of a swing trading strategy over the past year.

5. **Alerts and Notifications:** Traders can set up price alerts, sound alerts, and email notifications to stay informed about market movements and important events.

Example: A cryptocurrency trader can configure an alert to notify them when Bitcoin's price reaches a specific level.

6. **One-Click Trading:** MT4 offers one-click trading for fast order execution. Traders can quickly enter and exit positions with a single mouse click.

Example: A day trader in the futures market can use one-click trading in MT4 to swiftly capitalize on short-term price movements.

Significance of MetaTrader 4 (MT4) in Trading:

MetaTrader 4 has achieved immense significance in the trading industry for several reasons:

1. **Global Adoption:** MT4 is supported by a vast network of brokers worldwide, making it accessible to traders in various regions and asset classes.

2. **Community and Marketplace:** Traders can access a vibrant online community and a marketplace where they can find thousands of custom indicators, EAs, and scripts created by other users.

3. **Reliability and Stability:** MT4 is known for its stability and reliability, with minimal downtime and a robust infrastructure.

4. **Compatibility:** The platform is compatible with Windows, macOS, iOS, and Android devices, allowing traders to access their accounts from anywhere.

Example of Using MetaTrader 4 (MT4):

Suppose you are a cryptocurrency trader interested in Bitcoin. You have downloaded and installed MetaTrader 4 (MT4) from your chosen broker's website. After logging in to your trading account within the platform, you access the Bitcoin (BTC/USD) chart.

Using MT4's technical analysis tools, you analyze the recent price movement of Bitcoin and identify a potential support level at $45,000. To capitalize on a potential price bounce from this level, you decide to place a buy order with a stop-loss set at $44,500.

You then apply a custom indicator that you downloaded from the MT4 marketplace to confirm your entry point. If the indicator generates a buy signal based on your predefined criteria, MT4 will execute your trade automatically.

Key Considerations:

- While MT4 offers many advantages, traders should be aware of its limitations, such as its outdated interface compared to more modern platforms like MetaTrader 5 (MT5).

- It is crucial to choose a reputable broker that offers MT4 as a trading platform, as the quality of service and available features may vary among brokers.

In conclusion, MetaTrader 4 (MT4) is a versatile and widely used trading platform known for its accessibility, advanced charting, automated trading capabilities, and supportive online community.

Chapter 46

Trading Through TradingView

TradingView is a popular and versatile web-based platform that caters to traders and investors across various financial markets. Known for its intuitive interface, advanced charting capabilities, and extensive library of technical analysis tools, TradingView has gained widespread adoption among traders worldwide. In this chapter, we will explore the features, functionalities, and significance of TradingView as a trading platform, accompanied by detailed explanations and real-world examples.

Features and Functionalities of TradingView:

1. **Advanced Charting:** TradingView offers highly customizable and interactive charts with a wide range of timeframes, chart types (candlestick, line, bar), and drawing tools. Traders can apply technical indicators, trendlines, and other analysis tools to conduct in-depth technical analysis.

Example: A cryptocurrency trader can use TradingView's charts to analyze the price movements of Ethereum (ETH/USD) and identify potential support and resistance levels.

2. **Indicator Library:** TradingView provides access to a vast library of technical indicators created by the platform's users. Traders can explore and use a wide array of indicators to develop their trading strategies.

Example: A stock trader can add the Bollinger Bands and MACD indicators to their TradingView chart to assess stock price volatility and potential trend reversals.

3. **Custom Scripting:** For more advanced traders and developers, TradingView allows the creation of custom scripts using Pine Script,

a domain-specific scripting language. Traders can design their own indicators and strategies.

Example: A forex trader can develop a custom Pine Script indicator that combines multiple moving averages to generate buy and sell signals.

4. **Social and Community Features:** TradingView offers a social network-like experience, allowing traders to follow other users, share trading ideas, and engage in discussions about market trends and strategies.

Example: A commodities trader can follow an experienced TradingView user who regularly posts analysis and trade setups for gold and silver.

5. **Paper Trading:** TradingView offers a paper trading feature that allows traders to practice and test their strategies in a risk-free virtual environment before trading with real capital.

Example: A futures trader can simulate trading crude oil futures on TradingView's paper trading platform to gain confidence and refine their strategy.

6. **Broker Integration:** TradingView integrates with various brokerage platforms, enabling traders to execute orders directly from the TradingView interface with supported brokers.

Significance of Trading Through TradingView:

Trading through TradingView holds several advantages and significance for traders:

1. **Accessibility:** TradingView is a web-based platform, meaning traders can access it from any device with an internet connection. This accessibility enhances convenience and flexibility.

2. **Community Collaboration:** Traders can benefit from the shared knowledge and trading ideas within the TradingView community.

Engaging with other traders can lead to insights and improved trading strategies.

3. **Customization:** TradingView's extensive customization options allow traders to tailor their charts, indicators, and layouts to suit their preferences and trading styles.

Example of Trading Through TradingView:

Suppose you are a forex trader interested in trading the EUR/USD currency pair. You access TradingView's platform, create a chart for EUR/USD, and apply technical indicators such as the Relative Strength Index (RSI) and the Moving Average Convergence Divergence (MACD) to your chart for analysis.

After conducting your technical analysis, you identify a potential entry point to buy EUR/USD at a support level. You set your stop-loss and take-profit levels directly on the TradingView chart. When you are ready to execute the trade, you connect TradingView to your brokerage account, and the order is executed seamlessly through the platform.

Key Considerations:

- While TradingView offers many features for free, some advanced features may require a subscription or premium membership.

- Traders should ensure that their chosen brokerage platform is compatible with TradingView if they intend to execute trades directly from the platform.

In conclusion, TradingView is a powerful and user-friendly trading platform that appeals to traders and investors in various financial markets. Its extensive charting tools, indicator library, social features, and broker integration make it a valuable resource for traders looking to conduct technical analysis, develop strategies, and execute trades efficiently. Whether you are a novice or experienced trader, TradingView provides a versatile and collaborative environment for trading and analysis.

Chapter 47

Money Management

Money management is a critical aspect of trading that focuses on the prudent allocation and preservation of capital. It encompasses a set of rules and strategies designed to control risk, minimize losses, and optimize profits. Successful traders understand that effective money management is just as important as their trading strategy. In this chapter, we will delve into the concept of money management in trading, its key principles, and provide detailed explanations along with real-world examples.

The Importance of Money Management:

Effective money management is paramount for traders for several reasons:

1. **Risk Mitigation:** Money management techniques help traders protect their trading capital from significant losses, ensuring they have the resources to continue trading.

2. **Emotional Control:** Proper money management reduces the emotional stress associated with trading, preventing impulsive decisions driven by fear or greed.

3. **Consistency:** A consistent money management strategy helps traders maintain a structured approach to trading, avoiding large drawdowns that can disrupt their overall strategy.

Key Principles of Money Management:

1. **Risk Per Trade:** Determine the maximum percentage of your trading capital you are willing to risk on a single trade. This percentage should align with your risk tolerance and trading strategy.

Example: If you have a $10,000 trading account and are willing to risk 2% per trade, your maximum risk per trade is $200.

2. **Position Sizing:** Calculate the position size for each trade based on the distance from your entry point to your stop-loss level. Position size should be adjusted to keep your risk consistent.

Example: If you enter a stock trade at $50 and your stop loss is at $48, with a $200 maximum risk, you can calculate your position size as ($50 - $48) / $2 = 100 shares.

3. **Stop-Loss Orders:** Always use stop-loss orders to limit potential losses on each trade. Set your stop-loss level at a point that aligns with your risk per trade.

Example: If you enter a forex trade at 1.1200 and are willing to risk 30 pips (0.0030) with a $200 maximum risk, your stop loss should be set at 1.1170.

4. **Risk-Reward Ratio:** Assess the potential reward compared to the risk for each trade. A favorable risk-reward ratio ensures that potential gains outweigh potential losses.

Example: If you enter a trade with a 2:1 risk-reward ratio, you are risking $100 to potentially gain $200.

5. **Diversification:** Spread your trading capital across multiple trades or assets to reduce the impact of a single loss on your overall capital.

Example: Instead of investing all your capital in a single stock, allocate it across various stocks, bonds, and commodities.

Money Management in Action:

Imagine you are a forex trader looking to enter a trade in the EUR/USD currency pair. You have a trading account with a balance of $10,000 and are willing to risk 2% of your capital per trade. Your analysis suggests that the potential entry point for a long trade is at 1.1200, and you set your stop loss at 1.1150.

With a 2% risk per trade, your maximum risk for this trade is $200 ($10,000 * 0.02). You calculate your position size based on the distance between your entry point (1.1200) and stop loss (1.1150), which is 50 pips (0.0050).

Position size = Maximum risk / Distance to stop loss = $200 / 50 pips = $4 per pip

Since you are trading the EUR/USD, where each pip represents $10 per standard lot, you can calculate your position size as $4 / $10 per pip = 0.4 standard lots.

By following this money management strategy, you ensure that your risk per trade is controlled, allowing you to trade with discipline and protect your capital.

Key Considerations:

- Money management should be an integral part of your trading plan, and it is essential to stick to your predefined risk parameters.

- Over-leveraging, or risking too much capital on a single trade, can lead to significant losses. Leverage should be used cautiously and in line with your risk tolerance.

- Regularly review and adjust your money management strategies as your trading capital, objectives, and market conditions change.

In conclusion, money management is a fundamental pillar of successful trading. By following key principles such as risk per trade, position sizing, stop-loss orders, risk-reward ratios, and diversification, traders can protect their capital and enhance their chances of consistent profitability in the dynamic world of financial markets.

Chapter 48

Trade Analysis

Trade analysis is a critical component of a trader's decision-making process, involving the assessment of potential trade opportunities to determine their viability and risk-reward profile. It encompasses both technical and fundamental analysis, as well as the evaluation of market conditions and factors that may impact a trade. In this chapter, we will explore the concept of trade analysis, its key elements, and provide detailed explanations along with real-world examples.

Key Elements of Trade Analysis:

1. **Technical Analysis:** Technical analysis involves the study of historical price charts and patterns to forecast future price movements. Traders use technical indicators, chart patterns, and trend analysis to identify potential entry and exit points for trades.

Example: A stock trader may analyze a company's stock chart to identify a bullish trend indicated by higher highs and higher lows, along with support and resistance levels.

2. **Fundamental Analysis:** Fundamental analysis focuses on assessing the underlying factors that influence an asset's value. This includes examining economic data, financial reports, news events, and other fundamental indicators relevant to the asset being traded.

Example: A forex trader may consider the economic data of a country, such as GDP growth, inflation rates, and interest rates, to make informed decisions about trading a currency pair.

3. **Risk Management:** Evaluating the risk associated with a trade is a crucial aspect of trade analysis. Traders assess potential losses, set stop-loss orders, and determine the appropriate position size to manage risk effectively.

208

Example: A cryptocurrency trader may calculate the maximum amount they are willing to risk on a trade and set a stop-loss order accordingly to limit potential losses.

4. **Market Conditions:** Traders consider the current market environment, including volatility, liquidity, and overall sentiment. Market conditions can affect trade execution and strategy.

Example: A commodities trader may adapt their strategy based on changing market conditions, such as increased volatility in the oil market due to geopolitical events.

5. **News and Events:** Keeping track of news and events that may impact the asset being traded is essential. Unexpected news releases, economic events, or corporate earnings reports can have a significant influence on prices.

Example: An options trader may monitor the earnings calendar to anticipate price movements in a particular stock after the release of quarterly earnings.

Trade Analysis in Action:

Suppose you are a trader interested in the stock market, and you have identified a potential trade opportunity in Company XYZ. After conducting trade analysis, you gather the following information:

- **Technical Analysis:** The stock is in an uptrend, with consistent higher highs and higher lows. It recently bounced off a well-defined support level, suggesting a potential entry point.

- **Fundamental Analysis:** Company XYZ has released positive earnings reports, indicating strong financial performance. Additionally, the industry sector in which the company operates is showing signs of growth.

- **Risk Management:** You determine that your maximum acceptable risk for this trade is 2% of your trading capital. You set a stop-loss order at a level that aligns with this risk tolerance.

- **Market Conditions:** The broader market is experiencing increased volatility due to economic uncertainties, which may impact the stock's price movement.

- **News and Events:** There are no significant pending news or earnings releases for Company XYZ that could directly affect the stock in the short term.

Based on this trade analysis, you decide to enter a long position in Company XYZ, with a clear understanding of your entry and exit points, risk parameters, and the overall market context.

Key Considerations:

- Trade analysis is an ongoing process, and traders should continually monitor their positions and adjust their strategies as new information becomes available.

- Combining technical and fundamental analysis can provide a more comprehensive view of potential trade opportunities.

- Effective trade analysis requires discipline and adherence to predetermined risk management rules.

In conclusion, trade analysis is an essential skill for traders seeking to make informed and strategic decisions in the financial markets. By employing technical and fundamental analysis, managing risk effectively, and staying informed about market conditions and news events, traders can enhance their ability to identify and execute successful trades.

Chapter 49

Protect Your Account

Protecting your trading account is a paramount concern for traders of all levels. Whether you are a beginner or an experienced trader, safeguarding your capital is crucial for long-term success in the financial markets. In this chapter, we will delve into the strategies, practices, and key considerations for protecting your trading account, accompanied by detailed explanations and real-world examples.

Strategies for Protecting Your Trading Account:

1. **Risk Management:** Implementing a sound risk management strategy is the foundation of account protection. This includes setting a maximum risk per trade, calculating position sizes, and using stop-loss orders to limit potential losses. By defining your risk parameters and sticking to them, you ensure that no single trade can severely deplete your account.

Example: If your trading capital is $10,000 and you are willing to risk 2% per trade, your maximum risk per trade should not exceed $200.

2. **Diversification:** Avoid overconcentration in a single asset or trading position. Diversifying your portfolio across different assets, markets, and trading strategies can help reduce the impact of a single loss on your overall account.

Example: Instead of investing all your capital in one stock, allocate it across stocks, bonds, commodities, and forex.

3. **Stop-Loss Orders:** Always use stop-loss orders to protect your trades. These orders automatically close a position when the market moves against you, limiting potential losses. Ensure that your stop-loss levels are set based on your risk tolerance and analysis.

Example: If you enter a forex trade at 1.1200 and are willing to risk 30 pips with a $200 maximum risk, your stop loss should be set at 1.1170.

4. **Take-Profit Orders:** In addition to stop-loss orders, use take-profit orders to lock in profits at predefined levels. This prevents a winning trade from turning into a losing one if the market reverses.

Example: If you enter a stock trade at $50 and expect a target price of $55, you can set a take-profit order at $55.

5. **Risk-Reward Ratio:** Assess the potential reward compared to the risk for each trade. Favorable risk-reward ratios ensure that potential gains outweigh potential losses.

Example: If you enter a trade with a 3:1 risk-reward ratio, you are risking $100 to potentially gain $300.

6. **Regular Monitoring:** Continuously monitor your open positions, market conditions, and news events. Be prepared to adjust or exit trades if new information or adverse market developments arise.

Example: A cryptocurrency trader keeps a close eye on regulatory news and updates that may impact the value of the assets in their portfolio.

Key Considerations for Account Protection:

1. **Emotional Discipline:** Emotional trading decisions, such as revenge trading after a loss or chasing gains, can lead to account depletion. Maintain emotional discipline and stick to your trading plan.

Example: A trader experiences a losing streak but avoids the temptation to increase position sizes in an attempt to recover losses.

2. **Education and Training:** Continuous learning and improving your trading skills are essential for account protection. Stay updated on market developments, trading strategies, and risk management techniques.

Example: A novice trader invests time in learning technical analysis and risk management principles before committing significant capital to trading.

3. **Adaptability:** Markets are dynamic and can change rapidly. Be adaptable and willing to adjust your trading strategies and risk parameters as market conditions evolve.

Example: A commodities trader modifies their trading strategy when they notice increased market volatility due to geopolitical events.

4. **Account Monitoring Tools:** Utilize trading platform features and external tools to monitor your account's performance, track trades, and receive alerts about significant market movements.

Example: An options trader sets up notifications on their trading platform to receive real-time alerts when certain price levels are reached.

In conclusion, protecting your trading account is a fundamental aspect of successful trading. By implementing robust risk management practices, diversifying your portfolio, using stop-loss and take-profit orders, and maintaining emotional discipline, you can safeguard your capital and ensure longevity in the world of financial markets. Continual learning and adaptability further strengthen your ability to protect your trading account and achieve trading success.

Chapter 50

The Importance of Recording Historical Trades

Recording and analyzing historical trades is an essential practice for traders seeking to improve their performance and achieve long-term success in the financial markets. Maintaining a comprehensive trading journal allows traders to gain insights, identify strengths and weaknesses, and make data-driven decisions. In this chapter, we will explore the significance of recording historical trades, the elements of an effective trading journal, and provide detailed explanations along with real-world examples.

The Significance of Recording Historical Trades:

1. **Self-Reflection and Improvement:** A trading journal serves as a self-reflective tool, enabling traders to review past trades objectively. By analyzing what went right and wrong, traders can continuously improve their skills and strategies.

Example: A forex trader reviews their trading journal and notices a recurring pattern of impulsive entries during volatile market hours. Recognizing this, they can work on better managing their emotions.

2. **Objective Analysis:** Emotions often cloud judgment during trading. A trading journal provides an objective record of trades, helping traders separate emotions from analysis and decision-making.

Example: An options trader who felt anxious during a trade can review their journal and see if their anxiety correlated with specific market conditions or trade outcomes.

3. **Pattern Recognition:** Tracking historical trades allows traders to identify patterns in their trading behavior, such as overtrading, risk management lapses, or consistent errors. Recognizing these patterns can lead to targeted improvements.

Example: A commodities trader identifies a pattern of not adhering to predetermined stop-loss levels. This awareness prompts them to focus on discipline and risk management.

4. **Strategy Evaluation:** A trading journal helps traders assess the effectiveness of their trading strategies over time. By analyzing historical performance, traders can refine or adapt their strategies as market conditions change.

Example: A stock trader reviews their journal and notices that their swing trading strategy is consistently profitable in specific sectors but less so in others. This insight leads them to refine their strategy for better results.

5. **Accountability:** A trading journal holds traders accountable for their decisions. It helps ensure that they follow their trading plan and adhere to risk management rules consistently.

Example: A cryptocurrency trader reviews their journal and acknowledges instances of deviating from their risk parameters. This realization reinforces the importance of discipline.

Elements of an Effective Trading Journal:

1. **Trade Details:** Record the date and time of each trade, the asset traded, entry and exit prices, position size, and the direction (buy or sell).

2. **Trading Plan:** Include details of your trading plan for each trade, including the rationale behind the trade, entry and exit criteria, and the risk-reward ratio.

3. **Emotional State:** Describe your emotional state before, during, and after the trade. Note any anxiety, confidence, or fear.

4. **Market Conditions:** Document the prevailing market conditions, such as volatility, news events, or significant price levels, that may have influenced your trade.

5. **Risk Management:** Record the risk parameters of each trade, including the percentage of capital risked, stop-loss and take-profit levels, and any adjustments made during the trade.

6. **Trade Outcome:** Note whether the trade was a win, loss, or breakeven. Include details of any slippage or execution issues.

Example of the Importance of Recording Historical Trades:

Suppose you are a futures trader specializing in trading gold contracts. You have been consistently profitable but want to further improve your performance. You decide to maintain a detailed trading journal to gain insights.

After a few months, you review your journal and notice a pattern: your winning trades consistently have a risk-reward ratio of 1:2 or better, while your losing trades often result from impulsive decisions during volatile market hours. Recognizing this, you decide to refine your trading strategy by adhering to stricter risk-reward ratios and avoiding trading during high volatility periods.

As a result, your trading performance improves significantly, and you become more consistent in your profitability.

Key Considerations:

- Recording historical trades should be an ongoing practice. Continuously update your trading journal with each trade to maintain a complete record.

- Use technology to your advantage. Many trading platforms offer built-in tools for recording trades, but you can also use spreadsheet software or dedicated journaling apps.

In conclusion, recording and analyzing historical trades is an invaluable practice for traders seeking to refine their skills and achieve long-term success in the financial markets.

Chapter 51

Batting Average and Win/Loss Ratio

Batting average and win/loss ratio are two crucial metrics that traders use to assess the effectiveness of their trading strategies and their overall trading performance. These metrics provide valuable insights into a trader's ability to profit from their trades and manage risk effectively. In this chapter, we will explore the concepts of batting average and win/loss ratio, their significance, how to calculate them, and provide detailed explanations along with real-world examples.

Batting Average:

Batting average, also known as the win rate or success rate, measures the percentage of winning trades relative to the total number of trades executed. It is a key indicator of a trader's ability to make profitable decisions and execute successful trades.

Calculation of Batting Average:

Batting Average (%) = (Number of Winning Trades / Total Number of Trades) x 100

For example, if a trader has executed 50 trades and 30 of them were winners, their batting average would be:

Batting Average = (30 / 50) x 100 = 60%

A batting average of 60% indicates that the trader has won 60% of their trades.

Significance of Batting Average:

A high batting average suggests that a trader is making more winning trades than losing ones, which can boost their confidence and reinforce their trading strategy. However, a high batting average alone does not guarantee profitability. It is essential to consider other factors, such as risk-reward ratios and overall risk management, to assess the overall profitability of a trading strategy.

Win/Loss Ratio:

The win/loss ratio, also known as the risk-reward ratio, quantifies the relationship between the potential reward and the risk taken on each trade. It measures the amount of profit generated for every dollar of potential loss.

Calculation of Win/Loss Ratio:

Win/Loss Ratio = (Total Winning Trade Profits) / (Total Losing Trade Losses)

For example, if a trader has generated $3,000 in profits from winning trades and incurred $1,500 in losses from losing trades, their win/loss ratio would be:

Win/Loss Ratio = $3,000 / $1,500 = 2

A win/loss ratio of 2 indicates that, on average, the trader earns $2 for every $1 they risk.

Significance of Win/Loss Ratio:

A favorable win/loss ratio suggests that the potential reward outweighs the risk, which can be an indication of a sound risk management strategy. Traders often aim for win/loss ratios greater than 1 to ensure that their winning trades compensate for their losing ones. However, a high win/loss ratio does not guarantee success if the batting average is low, as it may indicate that the trader is missing out on profitable opportunities.

Example of Batting Average and Win/Loss Ratio:

Consider a swing trader who has executed 30 trades over the past six months. Out of these 30 trades, 20 were winners, and 10 were losers.

1. **Batting Average:** The trader's batting average is calculated as follows:

Batting Average = (20 / 30) x 100 = 66.67%

The trader has a batting average of approximately 66.67%, indicating a relatively high success rate.

2. **Win/Loss Ratio:** To calculate the win/loss ratio, we consider the profits and losses from the trades:

Total Winning Trade Profits = $6,000 Total Losing Trade Losses = $3,000

Win/Loss Ratio = $6,000 / $3,000 = 2

The trader has a win/loss ratio of 2, meaning that, on average, they make $2 for every $1 they risk.

In this example, the trader has a high batting average and a favorable win/loss ratio, suggesting a strong trading performance with a higher probability of success. However, it is essential to consider other factors like position sizing, risk management, and overall profitability to make a comprehensive assessment of their trading strategy.

Key Considerations:

- A balance between a high batting average and a favorable win/loss ratio is often sought after by traders to achieve consistent profitability

- Traders should avoid solely focusing on one metric (e.g., batting average) at the expense of others, as a holistic approach to trading performance assessment is essential.

In conclusion, batting average and win/loss ratio are essential metrics that traders use to evaluate their trading performance. These metrics provide valuable insights into a trader's ability to make profitable decisions and manage risk effectively. By understanding and monitoring these metrics, traders can refine their trading strategies and work toward achieving consistent success in the financial markets.

Chapter 52

Trading Psychology

Trading psychology plays a pivotal role in a trader's success or failure in the financial markets. It encompasses the mental and emotional aspects of trading that influence decision-making, risk management, and overall trading performance. In this chapter, we will delve into the complexities of trading psychology, its significance, common psychological challenges faced by traders, and provide detailed explanations along with real-world examples.

Significance of Trading Psychology:

Trading can be emotionally taxing, as it involves real money and the potential for gains and losses. A trader's ability to control emotions and maintain a disciplined mindset is crucial for consistent profitability. Here are some key aspects of trading psychology and their significance:

1. **Emotional Discipline:** Emotions such as fear, greed, impatience, and overconfidence can lead to impulsive decisions and irrational trading behavior. Maintaining emotional discipline is essential for making objective, well-reasoned trading decisions.

Example: A trader experiences fear after a losing trade and decides to double their position size in the next trade, hoping to recoup losses quickly. This impulsive decision can lead to further losses.

2. **Patience and Discipline:** Successful trading often requires waiting for the right setups and adhering to a trading plan consistently. Impatience and a lack of discipline can lead to overtrading and poor decision-making.

Example: A day trader becomes impatient during a slow market day and starts making high-frequency trades without proper analysis, resulting in losses.

3. **Risk Management:** Emotional control is essential when managing risk. Traders must avoid taking excessive risks or deviating from their predetermined risk parameters due to fear or greed.

Example: A trader, driven by greed, decides to increase their position size beyond their risk tolerance, leading to a significant loss that they cannot afford.

4. **Resilience:** Traders often face losses and setbacks. Resilience is the ability to bounce back from losses, learn from mistakes, and continue trading with a positive mindset.

Example: After a series of losses, a trader takes time to review their trades, identify areas for improvement, and returns to trading with a renewed focus on discipline and risk management.

Common Psychological Challenges in Trading:

1. **Loss Aversion:** Traders often experience a stronger emotional response to losses than to gains. This can lead to holding losing positions for too long or closing winning positions prematurely.

2. **Overtrading:** The fear of missing out (FOMO) can lead to overtrading, where traders enter excessive positions, increasing the risk of losses.

3. **Confirmation Bias:** Traders may seek out information or analysis that confirms their existing beliefs or positions, leading to biased decision-making.

4. **Overconfidence:** Overconfidence can lead to a lack of caution and risk-taking behavior, resulting in losses.

5. **Revenge Trading:** After a significant loss, traders may engage in revenge trading, seeking to recover losses quickly, which often leads to further losses.

Strategies for Improving Trading Psychology:

1. **Mindfulness:** Practice mindfulness techniques to stay present and emotionally grounded while trading.

2. **Mental Preparation:** Prepare mentally before each trading session by reviewing your trading plan and setting clear objectives.

3. **Journaling:** Maintain a trading journal to track emotions, thoughts, and decisions for self-reflection and improvement.

4. **Risk Management:** Implement strict risk management rules to prevent impulsive decision-making and excessive risk-taking.

5. **Education:** Continuously educate yourself about trading psychology to better understand and manage your emotions.

Example of Trading Psychology:

Imagine a trader who has been consistently profitable in the past but recently experienced a series of losses. Frustration and self-doubt begin to affect their trading decisions. Instead of taking revenge trades or deviating from their strategy, they decide to step back from trading temporarily. During this break, they review their trading journal and identify patterns of overtrading and impulsive decisions. With a renewed focus on discipline and emotional control, they gradually regain their confidence and return to trading with a more disciplined mindset, leading to improved performance.

Key Considerations:

- Trading psychology is an ongoing journey. It requires constant self-awareness, self-discipline, and a commitment to continuous improvement.

- Seeking support from mentors, trading communities, or professional psychologists can be beneficial for traders struggling with psychological challenges.

Chapter 53

The Importance of Trading Psychology

Trading psychology stands as the cornerstone of successful trading in the financial markets. It encapsulates the intricate interplay of emotions, discipline, and mental fortitude that can make or break a trader's journey. In this chapter, we will delve into the profound significance of trading psychology, its far-reaching implications, common psychological pitfalls, and provide detailed explanations along with real-world examples.

The Profound Significance of Trading Psychology:

1. **Emotion as a Double-Edged Sword:** Emotions, such as fear and greed, are inherent to human nature and inevitably seep into trading decisions. How traders manage these emotions can greatly impact their outcomes. A lack of emotional control can lead to impulsive decisions, excessive risk-taking, and ultimately, losses.

Example: Consider a trader who, driven by fear, prematurely exits a winning position to secure a small profit, missing out on substantial gains if they had stuck to their original plan.

2. **Discipline as the Bedrock:** Discipline is the linchpin of a trader's success. It involves adhering to a well-thought-out trading plan, patiently waiting for the right opportunities, and maintaining consistency in risk management. A lack of discipline can result in overtrading, deviation from a proven strategy, and significant losses.

Example: An impulsive trader, eager to recover recent losses, takes on multiple trades in quick succession, disregarding risk parameters and ending up with a substantial drawdown.

3. **Psychological Pitfalls and Cognitive Biases:** Trading is rife with cognitive biases, including confirmation bias (seeking information that confirms existing beliefs) and overconfidence (overestimating

one's abilities). These biases can lead to skewed perceptions and suboptimal decision-making.

Example: A trader, influenced by confirmation bias, dismisses warning signs of a potential market reversal because they only seek out analysis that supports their bullish outlook.

4. **Managing Adversity and Losses:** Every trader encounters losses and setbacks. How one copes with these inevitable challenges, learns from mistakes, and maintains psychological resilience can determine their ultimate success.

Example: After a series of losses, a trader takes time for introspection, identifies weaknesses in their strategy, and refines their approach, ultimately recovering and achieving consistent profitability.

Strategies for Mastering Trading Psychology:

1. **Mindfulness and Emotional Awareness:** Practicing mindfulness techniques helps traders stay in the present moment, fostering emotional control and reducing impulsive behavior.

2. **Mental Preparation:** Before each trading session, take time to mentally prepare by reviewing your trading plan, setting clear objectives, and acknowledging potential emotional triggers.

3. **Journaling:** A trading journal serves as a mirror to your trading psyche. Documenting your emotions, thoughts, and decisions provides invaluable self-awareness and a basis for improvement.

4. **Risk Management:** Implement stringent risk management rules and stick to them rigorously. This includes setting stop-loss orders and determining position sizes based on your risk tolerance.

5. **Continual Education:** Invest time in learning about trading psychology to gain a deeper understanding of your emotional triggers and cognitive biases.

Example of Trading Psychology:

Imagine a trader who, after experiencing a series of losses, finds their confidence shattered. They are haunted by self-doubt, fearing that they are no longer capable of making profitable trades. Instead of succumbing to emotional turmoil, they seek guidance from a trading mentor who specializes in psychology. Through introspection, mindfulness, and disciplined practice, the trader gradually rebuilds their confidence and emotional resilience. They learn to embrace losses as valuable lessons and ultimately regain their footing in the markets.

Key Considerations:

- Trading psychology is a journey, not a destination. It requires constant self-awareness, self-discipline, and a commitment to personal growth.

- Traders should not hesitate to seek support from mentors, trading communities, or even professional psychologists when struggling with psychological challenges.

In conclusion, the importance of trading psychology cannot be overstated. It is the invisible force that underpins every trading decision, guiding traders through the treacherous terrain of financial markets. By recognizing the significance of emotional control, discipline, and psychological resilience, traders can unlock their true potential and embark on a path toward consistent profitability and trading success.

Chapter 54

Loss Aversion

Loss aversion is a powerful psychological phenomenon that significantly influences trading behavior and decision-making in the financial markets. It refers to the cognitive bias where individuals feel the pain of losses more intensely than the pleasure of equivalent gains. In this chapter, we will explore the concept of loss aversion, its profound impact on traders, common manifestations, and provide detailed explanations along with real-world examples.

Understanding Loss Aversion:

Loss aversion is rooted in human psychology and was first introduced by psychologists Amos Tversky and Daniel Kahneman in their groundbreaking prospect theory. It reveals that the emotional impact of a loss is roughly twice as powerful as the pleasure derived from an equivalent gain.

The Impact of Loss Aversion on Traders:

1. **Hesitation to Cut Losses:** Loss-averse traders often hesitate to cut their losing positions, hoping for a turnaround even when market conditions suggest otherwise. This can lead to mounting losses and a reluctance to accept defeat.

Example: A trader refuses to place a stop-loss order on a position, believing that the market will eventually move in their favor. As the loss deepens, they find it increasingly difficult to exit the trade.

2. **Quick Profit-Taking:** Conversely, traders may exhibit a tendency to quickly take profits in winning trades to avoid the possibility of losing those gains. This behavior can lead to prematurely closing out winning positions and missing out on potential larger profits.

226

Example: A trader, upon seeing a modest profit in a trade, hastily closes the position to lock in the gain. The market continues to move in their favor, ultimately resulting in a missed opportunity for more significant profit.

3. **Avoiding Risk:** Loss aversion can lead traders to avoid taking risks, even when the potential reward justifies it. They may opt for safer, less volatile assets or overly conservative positions to minimize the perceived risk of loss.

Example: A trader, despite strong technical indicators pointing to a high-probability trade, decides not to enter because they are afraid of potential losses.

4. **Chasing Losses:** Loss-averse traders are susceptible to chasing losses by increasing position sizes or taking higher risks to recover previous losses quickly. This often exacerbates losses and increases the emotional toll.

Example: After a significant loss, a trader decides to double their position size in the next trade, hoping to recoup their losses in a single trade. If the trade goes against them, it results in an even more substantial loss.

Mitigating the Impact of Loss Aversion:

1. **Implement Strict Risk Management:** By setting predetermined stop-loss orders and adhering to them, traders can limit potential losses and mitigate the emotional impact of losses.

2. **Focus on Long-Term Goals:** Traders should maintain a long-term perspective and recognize that losses are part of the trading journey. Accepting that not every trade will be a winner can help reduce the emotional toll of losses.

3. **Keep a Trading Journal:** Maintaining a detailed trading journal can provide a clear record of trading decisions and their outcomes. It helps traders objectively evaluate their trades and identify areas for improvement.

227

4. **Practice Mindfulness:** Mindfulness techniques can help traders stay present and make rational decisions, reducing impulsive behavior driven by loss aversion.

Example of Loss Aversion in Trading:

Imagine a trader who has a winning position in a stock that has increased by 20%. They are feeling content with their profit but are worried about losing those gains. Fearing a potential market reversal, they decide to close the trade prematurely, locking in a 20% gain. However, the stock continues to surge, eventually reaching a 50% gain. The trader, influenced by loss aversion, missed out on the opportunity for a more substantial profit due to their hesitancy to hold the position.

Key Considerations:

- Recognizing and understanding loss aversion is the first step in mitigating its impact on trading decisions.

- Traders should focus on developing a disciplined approach to risk management and maintaining a rational, long-term perspective.

In conclusion, loss aversion is a potent psychological bias that affects traders across all experience levels. It can lead to suboptimal trading decisions, including hesitating to cut losses, prematurely taking profits, and avoiding risk. Traders must be aware of the influence of loss aversion and employ strategies to mitigate its effects, allowing them to make more rational and profitable trading decisions in the financial markets.

Chapter 55

Endowment Effect

The endowment effect is a cognitive bias that profoundly influences trading behavior and decision-making in the financial markets. It occurs when individuals assign a higher value to assets or securities they already possess simply because they own them. In this chapter, we will explore the concept of the endowment effect, its impact on traders, common manifestations, and provide detailed explanations along with real-world examples.

Understanding the Endowment Effect:

The endowment effect is a psychological phenomenon that challenges the traditional economic theory of rational decision-making. It was first introduced by behavioral economists Richard Thaler, Daniel Kahneman, and Jack Knetsch. It suggests that people tend to overvalue items they own and are more reluctant to part with them than they would be to acquire the same items.

The Impact of the Endowment Effect on Traders:

1. **Hesitation to Sell Winning Positions:** Traders affected by the endowment effect may be hesitant to sell winning positions, even when market conditions suggest it is the rational choice. This reluctance to part with profitable assets can lead to missed opportunities for profit-taking.

Example: A trader holds a stock that has doubled in value since their purchase. Despite indications that the stock may be overvalued and could experience a correction, they are emotionally attached to it and decide to hold on, missing out on potential gains.

2. **Irrational Resistance to Cutting Losses:** The endowment effect can also manifest in traders' reluctance to cut losses on positions that have turned against them. They may hold onto losing positions in the hope that the market will eventually turn in their favor.

Example: A trader is holding a losing position in a cryptocurrency. Instead of accepting the loss and exiting the trade, they continue to hold onto the asset, hoping for a reversal, even as the price continues to decline.

3. **Excessive Risk Aversion:** Traders influenced by the endowment effect may become excessively risk-averse, particularly when it comes to the assets they already own. They may avoid diversifying their portfolios or exploring new trading opportunities due to an emotional attachment to their existing holdings.

Example: A trader, who has been successful trading a specific currency pair, refuses to explore other currency pairs or asset classes, missing out on potential profitable trades.

4. **Reluctance to Reevaluate:** Traders may resist reevaluating their existing positions and investment strategies, even when market conditions or new information warrant a reassessment. This can lead to inflexibility in response to changing market dynamics.

Example: A trader who has held a particular stock for years is resistant to reconsidering their investment thesis, even as the company faces changing industry trends and competitive pressures.

Mitigating the Impact of the Endowment Effect:

1. **Regular Portfolio Review:** Traders should conduct regular portfolio reviews to objectively assess the performance and potential of their existing holdings.

2. **Adopt a Systematic Approach:** Develop and follow a systematic trading strategy that includes predefined entry and exit criteria to minimize the influence of emotional attachment.

3. **Diversify Portfolio:** Diversification can help reduce the emotional attachment to individual assets, as traders become less reliant on any single position.

4. **Seek External Opinions:** Consulting with mentors or trusted advisors can provide an external perspective and help traders overcome the endowment effect.

Example of the Endowment Effect in Trading:

Consider a trader who has held a particular technology stock for several years, and it has become a significant portion of their portfolio. Despite recent concerns about the company's future growth prospects and increasing competition, the trader is emotionally attached to the stock. They resist selling the position and fail to consider reallocating their funds to potentially more promising opportunities in the market. Their reluctance to part with the stock stems from the endowment effect, as they overvalue it due to their ownership.

Key Considerations:

- Recognizing the endowment effect is essential for traders seeking to make rational, objective decisions in the financial markets.

- Implementing a systematic approach to trading and regularly reviewing one's portfolio can help mitigate the impact of this cognitive bias.

In conclusion, the endowment effect is a cognitive bias that can significantly influence trading decisions and hinder traders from making rational choices in the financial markets. By understanding the endowment effect and implementing strategies to counteract its influence, traders can make more objective and profitable trading decisions, ultimately enhancing their success in the world of trading and investing.

Chapter 56

Status Quo Bias

Status quo bias is a powerful cognitive bias that exerts a significant influence on trading behavior and decision-making in the financial markets. This bias reflects a preference for the current state of affairs and an aversion to change, even when change may be rational or beneficial. In this chapter, we will delve into the concept of status quo bias, its impact on traders, common manifestations, and provide detailed explanations along with real-world examples.

Understanding Status Quo Bias:

Status quo bias is deeply rooted in human psychology and has been widely studied in the field of behavioral economics. It suggests that individuals tend to favor maintaining their current positions or holdings rather than making changes, even when the current situation may not be optimal.

The Impact of Status Quo Bias on Traders:

1. **Holding Losing Positions:** Traders affected by status quo bias may persistently hold onto losing positions, even when it is evident that the trades are unlikely to recover. This reluctance to cut losses can lead to significant portfolio drawdowns.

Example: A trader is holding a stock that has been in a downtrend for months. Instead of cutting their losses, they hold onto the position, hoping for a reversal, but the stock continues to decline.

2. **Avoiding Portfolio Rebalancing:** Status quo bias can deter traders from periodically rebalancing their portfolios, even when market conditions or asset performance indicate the need for adjustments. This can lead to overexposure to certain assets and increased risk.

Example: A trader's portfolio initially consisted of a balanced mix of stocks and bonds. However, as stock prices surged, they avoided selling stocks to rebalance their portfolio, leading to a disproportionate allocation to equities.

3. **Reluctance to Change Strategies:** Traders may adhere to outdated or underperforming trading strategies due to status quo bias, resisting the exploration of new approaches or tactics.

Example: A trader has been using a particular technical analysis method for years, even as it consistently fails to yield profitable results. They are reluctant to explore other strategies because they are comfortable with the status quo.

4. **Avoiding Exiting Winning Positions:** Status quo bias can also influence traders to avoid taking profits in winning positions. They may hold onto these positions out of a desire to maintain the status quo of a successful trade.

Example: A trader has a winning position in a currency pair that has reached their profit target. However, they decide to hold onto it in the hope of further gains, potentially exposing themselves to a reversal.

Mitigating the Impact of Status Quo Bias:

1. **Establish Clear Trading Rules:** Implementing predefined trading rules and strategies can help traders avoid the influence of status quo bias by promoting discipline and objective decision-making.

2. **Regular Portfolio Reassessment:** Periodically review your portfolio and trading strategies to ensure they align with your goals and market conditions.

3. **Seek External Opinions:** Consult with mentors, advisors, or trusted peers to gain external perspectives on your trading decisions and strategies.

4. **Embrace Change:** Embracing change and remaining open to new ideas and strategies can help traders overcome status quo bias and adapt to evolving market conditions.

Example of Status Quo Bias in Trading:

Imagine a trader who has been holding a losing position in a volatile cryptocurrency for an extended period. Despite significant losses and mounting evidence that the cryptocurrency's value is unlikely to recover, the trader resists selling the asset. They are influenced by status quo bias and prefer to maintain the current state of holding the cryptocurrency, hoping for a turnaround, even as their portfolio suffers.

Key Considerations:

- Status quo bias can have a detrimental impact on trading decisions and portfolio performance if left unchecked.

- Adopting a systematic approach to trading and embracing change are essential strategies for mitigating the influence of status quo bias.

In conclusion, status quo bias is a cognitive bias that can hinder traders from making rational and beneficial decisions in the financial markets. By recognizing the impact of this bias and actively working to counteract it, traders can enhance their ability to adapt to changing market conditions and improve their overall trading success.

Chapter 57

Anchoring Effect

The anchoring effect is a cognitive bias that holds considerable sway over trading decisions and behavior in the financial markets. It describes the tendency of individuals to rely heavily on the first piece of information they receive (the "anchor") when making subsequent decisions, even when that anchor may not be relevant or accurate. In this chapter, we will explore the concept of the anchoring effect, its impact on traders, common manifestations, and provide detailed explanations along with real-world examples.

Understanding the Anchoring Effect:

The anchoring effect is a cognitive bias that has been extensively studied in behavioral economics and psychology. It can lead individuals to make irrational decisions because they fixate on a specific piece of information, often without considering other relevant factors.

The Impact of the Anchoring Effect on Traders:

1. **Overvaluing Initial Price Points:** Traders influenced by the anchoring effect may place excessive importance on initial price levels when making trading decisions. For example, they may set take profit or stop-loss levels based solely on where the asset's price started, regardless of current market conditions.

Example: A trader buys a stock at $50 per share. They set a take-profit order at $55 because that was the stock's price when they entered the trade. They fail to consider changes in market sentiment or technical factors that could affect the stock's movement.

2. **Inaccurate Price Expectations:** The anchoring effect can lead traders to develop unrealistic price expectations based on historical prices or past performance. This can result in trades that are out of sync with the current market dynamics.

Example: A trader becomes anchored to a cryptocurrency that recently reached an all-time high of $1,000. They buy the cryptocurrency at $800, expecting it to return to its previous peak, even though market conditions have changed.

3. **Resistance to Price Corrections:** Traders influenced by the anchoring effect may resist acknowledging price corrections or reversals when the market moves against their positions. They hold onto losing positions in the hope that prices will return to their anchored reference points.

Example: A trader purchases a commodity futures contract at a historically high price. As the price begins to decline, they are anchored to the initial high point and refuse to cut their losses, hoping for a rebound.

4. **Inefficient Use of Technical Analysis:** Traders may overemphasize past price levels or patterns, relying on them as anchors for future price predictions. This can lead to biased interpretations of technical analysis and suboptimal trading decisions.

Example: A trader uses a moving average crossover strategy but bases their buy and sell signals solely on where the moving averages intersected in the past, without considering other technical indicators.

Mitigating the Impact of the Anchoring Effect:

1. **Diverse Sources of Information:** Gather information from a variety of sources and consider multiple factors when making trading decisions. Avoid fixating on a single price point or historical data.

2. **Clear Trading Plan:** Establish a well-defined trading plan that includes specific entry and exit criteria, based on a comprehensive analysis of current market conditions.

3. **Regular Review:** Continuously review and update your trading strategies to adapt to changing market dynamics, rather than clinging to past anchors.

4. **Mindful Decision-Making:** Practice mindfulness techniques to remain present and avoid impulsive decisions based on anchoring biases.

Example of the Anchoring Effect in Trading:

Imagine a trader who becomes anchored to the idea of a specific currency pair reaching parity (1:1 exchange rate) with another currency. The trader repeatedly buys the currency pair whenever it approaches close to the 1:1 level, believing that it will inevitably reach that point. However, market conditions, economic factors, and geopolitical events are not considered. The trader's fixation on the anchor of parity blinds them to the changing fundamentals, and they continue to incur losses as the currency pair never reaches their anchored reference point.

Key Considerations:

- Recognizing the anchoring effect is crucial for traders seeking to make rational and data-driven decisions in the financial markets.

- Employing a disciplined trading plan and remaining open to diverse sources of information can help mitigate the influence of the anchoring effect.

In conclusion, the anchoring effect is a cognitive bias that can lead traders astray by causing them to overly rely on specific anchor points or historical data when making trading decisions. By being aware of this bias and actively working to counteract it, traders can make more informed and objective decisions in the ever-changing landscape of financial markets.

Chapter 58

Confirmation Bias

Confirmation bias is a cognitive bias that significantly impacts trading behavior and decision-making in the financial markets. It refers to the tendency of individuals to seek out, interpret, and remember information in a way that confirms their existing beliefs or preconceptions while ignoring or downplaying contradictory information. In this chapter, we will delve into the concept of confirmation bias, its profound impact on traders, common manifestations, and provide detailed explanations along with real-world examples.

Understanding Confirmation Bias:

Confirmation bias is a well-documented cognitive bias that affects various aspects of human decision-making. Traders are particularly susceptible to this bias because they often form strong opinions and beliefs about the market or specific assets, which can lead to a selective interpretation of information.

The Impact of Confirmation Bias on Traders:

1. **Selective Information Gathering:** Traders influenced by confirmation bias tend to seek out information that aligns with their existing beliefs or trading positions. They may follow news sources, analysts, or market commentators who share their viewpoints while avoiding those who hold contrasting opinions.

Example: A trader who is bullish on a particular stock may actively seek out positive news articles and expert opinions that support their bullish outlook, ignoring any negative information about the stock's fundamentals.

2. **Misinterpreting Data:** Confirmation bias can lead traders to misinterpret data or technical indicators to fit their preconceived notions. They may see patterns or trends where none exist or downplay the significance of contradictory signals.

238

Example: A trader may disregard technical indicators suggesting a potential market reversal because they are convinced that their bullish position is correct, leading to losses.

3. **Overconfidence in Trading Strategies:** Traders may become overconfident in their chosen trading strategies and ignore signals that suggest a need for adjustment. This overconfidence can lead to excessive risk-taking and losses.

Example: A trader who has consistently used a specific trading strategy becomes overconfident in its effectiveness and refuses to consider alternative approaches, even as market conditions change.

4. **Reluctance to Accept Losses:** Confirmation bias can make it difficult for traders to accept losses or admit when they are wrong about a trade. They may hold onto losing positions, hoping for a reversal, rather than cutting their losses.

Example: A trader who is convinced that a currency pair will appreciate continues to hold the position despite a consistent decline in its value, refusing to accept the loss.

Mitigating the Impact of Confirmation Bias:

1. **Stay Open-Minded:** Actively seek out and consider diverse viewpoints and opinions, even if they contradict your existing beliefs or trading positions.

2. **Diversify Information Sources:** Obtain information from a variety of sources to reduce the risk of confirmation bias. Avoid relying solely on sources that align with your existing views.

3. **Keep a Trading Journal:** Maintain a detailed trading journal that documents your decisions, beliefs, and the reasons behind your trades. This can help you identify patterns of confirmation bias in your trading.

4. **Challenge Your Assumptions:** Continuously question and challenge your own assumptions and beliefs about the market. Be open to adjusting your trading strategies based on new information and changing conditions.

Example of Confirmation Bias in Trading:

Consider a trader who has a strong belief that a specific cryptocurrency will dominate the market due to its technological advancements. They actively seek out news articles and social media posts that support this belief, ignoring any information that raises concerns about the cryptocurrency's security vulnerabilities. This confirmation bias leads the trader to invest heavily in the cryptocurrency, despite mounting evidence that it may not be as secure as they think. Eventually, a security breach occurs, resulting in significant losses for the trader.

Key Considerations:

- Confirmation bias is a common cognitive bias that can have a detrimental impact on trading decisions and portfolio performance.

- Maintaining an open-minded approach to information and being willing to adapt to new insights is essential for mitigating the influence of confirmation bias.

In conclusion, confirmation bias is a cognitive bias that can distort traders' perceptions of the market and lead to biased decision-making. By recognizing the presence of confirmation bias and actively working to counteract it, traders can make more objective and informed trading decisions, ultimately enhancing their success in the financial markets.

Chapter 59

Be Aware of Important Changes

In the world of trading, staying informed about key developments and changes is essential for making informed decisions and managing risks effectively. The financial markets are dynamic and subject to various factors that can influence trading conditions. In this chapter, we will discuss some of the important changes that traders should be aware of, including regulatory changes, market shifts, and technological advancements, and provide detailed explanations along with real-world examples.

1. Regulatory Changes:

Regulations play a significant role in shaping the trading landscape. Governments and regulatory bodies regularly update and implement rules and policies aimed at maintaining market integrity and protecting investors. Traders should stay informed about regulatory changes that may impact their trading activities.

Example: In 2018, the European Union introduced the Markets in Financial Instruments Directive II (MiFID II), which brought significant changes to financial markets, including increased transparency requirements and stricter regulations on algorithmic trading.

2. Market Structure Shifts:

Market structures can evolve over time due to various factors, such as changes in market participants, technology, or economic conditions. Understanding these shifts is crucial for adapting trading strategies to current market dynamics.

Example: The rise of high-frequency trading (HFT) has significantly impacted market liquidity and execution speeds. Traders need to adapt to HFT-driven markets by employing appropriate strategies and risk management techniques.

3. Economic Events and Geopolitical Developments:

Economic data releases, geopolitical events, and central bank decisions can have a profound impact on financial markets. Being aware of scheduled announcements and their potential market effects is vital for traders.

Example: The decision of a central bank to change interest rates can lead to significant currency market movements. Traders who anticipate such events and their implications can position themselves accordingly.

4. Technological Advancements:

Advancements in technology continue to shape the trading landscape. From algorithmic trading to mobile trading apps, staying current with technological developments can provide traders with a competitive edge.

Example: The emergence of blockchain technology has led to the creation of cryptocurrency markets. Traders who adapt to this new asset class and its unique characteristics can capitalize on opportunities in the crypto space.

5. Risk Management Practices:

Risk management is a fundamental aspect of trading. Traders should regularly review and adapt their risk management strategies to account for changes in market conditions, portfolio size, and personal risk tolerance.

Example: A trader who initially risked 2% of their capital per trade may need to adjust this percentage if their portfolio size has grown or market volatility has increased.

6. Trading Psychology:

Emotions play a significant role in trading. Changes in market sentiment and personal emotions can affect decision-making. Traders should continuously work on their emotional discipline and mental resilience.

Example: During periods of market turmoil, fear and panic can lead to impulsive decisions. Traders who recognize their emotions and stick to their trading plan are better equipped to navigate challenging market conditions.

7. Global Economic Trends:

Understanding broader economic trends and their potential impact on various asset classes is essential for traders. Economic shifts, such as inflation, unemployment rates, and GDP growth, can influence investment decisions.

Example: A trader who anticipates rising inflation may adjust their portfolio by investing in assets that historically perform well during inflationary periods, such as commodities or inflation-protected securities.

8. Social Media and News Feeds:

Social media platforms and news feeds have become primary sources of market information and sentiment. Traders should be aware of the impact of news and social media on market volatility.

Example: A single tweet or news article can cause rapid price movements in certain assets. Traders who closely monitor news and social media channels can react swiftly to such events.

In conclusion, the world of trading is dynamic, and traders must stay informed about important changes and developments that can affect their trading activities. Whether it's regulatory updates, market shifts, technological advancements, or economic events, being aware and adaptable is crucial for success in trading. Staying informed, continuous learning, and maintaining a disciplined approach are key factors in achieving long-term trading goals.

Chapter 60

The Future is Now

"The Future is Now" in trading signifies that the financial markets are undergoing a rapid transformation driven by technological advancements and innovative approaches. Traders and investors are experiencing a shift in the way they engage with financial markets, access information, and execute trades. Here are some key aspects of "The Future is Now" in trading:

1. **Technology-Driven Trading:** High-frequency trading (HFT), algorithmic trading, and the use of advanced trading software have become commonplace. These technologies allow traders to execute orders at lightning speed, capitalize on market inefficiencies, and implement complex strategies.

2. **Big Data and Analytics:** The availability of vast amounts of financial data and the tools to analyze it are reshaping trading strategies. Machine learning and artificial intelligence are used to identify patterns, make predictions, and generate trading signals based on historical and real-time data.

3. **Automated Trading:** The future of trading is increasingly automated. Traders can use automated trading systems or trading bots to execute predefined strategies without constant manual intervention. These systems can trade 24/7, allowing access to global markets in real time.

4. **Alternative Assets:** Traditional asset classes like stocks and bonds are now joined by a range of alternative assets, including cryptocurrencies, commodities, and digital assets. These assets offer new trading opportunities and diversification options.

5. **Blockchain and Cryptocurrencies:** Blockchain technology has revolutionized the way financial transactions are conducted. Cryptocurrencies like Bitcoin and Ethereum have gained recognition as legitimate trading assets, opening up new avenues for speculation and investment.

6. **Decentralized Finance (DeFi):** DeFi platforms leverage blockchain technology to provide financial services such as lending, borrowing,

and trading without traditional intermediaries. DeFi is reshaping the landscape of traditional finance.

7. **Social Trading:** Social trading platforms enable traders to follow and replicate the trades of experienced investors. This collaborative approach allows less experienced traders to learn from experts and gain exposure to various trading strategies.

8. **Regulatory Changes:** Regulatory bodies are adapting to the changing landscape of trading. They are introducing new rules and guidelines to address the challenges and risks associated with modern trading practices.

9. **Globalization:** The global nature of financial markets means that traders can access a wide range of assets from around the world. Cross-border trading and international market integration are increasing.

10. **Democratization of Trading:** Online brokerage platforms and mobile apps have made trading accessible to a broader range of individuals. Retail traders can now compete in the same markets as institutional investors.

11. **Risk Management Tools:** Advanced risk management tools and features are available to traders. These tools help control risk by setting stop-loss orders, take-profit levels, and managing leverage.

12. **Education and Information:** The internet provides traders with access to a wealth of educational resources, market analysis, and financial news. Traders can stay informed and make data-driven decisions.

13. **Quantitative Trading:** Quantitative strategies, driven by mathematical models and statistical analysis, are increasingly prevalent. These strategies rely on algorithmic execution and can adapt to changing market conditions.

"The Future is Now" in trading highlights the need for traders to embrace technology, stay informed about market developments, and adapt to a rapidly changing environment. Success in trading requires a combination of technological proficiency, data analysis skills, and a deep understanding of the evolving financial landscape. Traders who can navigate this future are well-positioned to seize opportunities and manage risks effectively.

"The Future is Now" is a phrase that encapsulates the idea that the rapid pace of technological advancement and innovation is bringing the possibilities of the future into our present reality. It emphasizes that the future is not some distant point on the horizon but something that we are actively shaping and experiencing today. Here are some key points to consider when discussing the concept of "The Future is Now":

1. **Technological Advancement:** In recent decades, we've witnessed an unprecedented acceleration of technological progress. Breakthroughs in fields like artificial intelligence, biotechnology, renewable energy, and space exploration are transforming the way we live, work, and communicate.

2. **Innovation Across Industries:** Innovations are not confined to a single sector; they span across various industries. For example, the healthcare industry is revolutionized by telemedicine and personalized medicine, while the automotive industry is embracing electric and autonomous vehicles.

3. **Democratization of Information:** The internet and digital technologies have democratized access to information and education, enabling individuals and communities worldwide to participate in the global exchange of ideas and knowledge.

4. **Entrepreneurship and Startups:** Entrepreneurship is thriving, with startups and small companies driving innovation and disrupting traditional industries. Crowdfunding and venture capital have made it easier for innovators to bring their ideas to market.

5. **Sustainability and Green Technologies:** Concerns about climate change have accelerated the development and adoption of sustainable technologies. Renewable energy sources like solar and wind power are becoming increasingly accessible and affordable.

6. **Blockchain and Cryptocurrencies:** Blockchain technology and cryptocurrencies are reshaping the financial industry and offering new ways to transact, invest, and manage assets.

7. **Space Exploration:** Private companies are pioneering space exploration, making it possible for civilians to venture beyond Earth's atmosphere. Commercial space travel and colonization of other planets are becoming realistic possibilities.

8. **Biotechnology and Health:** Advances in genomics, gene editing, and regenerative medicine are revolutionizing healthcare, offering potential cures for previously untreatable diseases.
9. **Artificial Intelligence and Automation:** AI and automation are transforming industries by enhancing productivity and efficiency. They have applications in healthcare, finance, manufacturing, and more.
10. **Challenges and Ethical Considerations:** While technological advancements offer incredible opportunities, they also raise important ethical, privacy, and security concerns. Balancing innovation with responsible use is a critical aspect of navigating the future.
11. **Global Connectivity:** The world is becoming more interconnected than ever before, with global supply chains, digital communication, and social media connecting people across borders.
12. **Education and Lifelong Learning:** The rapid pace of change means that continuous learning and adaptability are essential. Lifelong learning is no longer an option but a necessity to thrive in the evolving job market.

In summary, "The Future is Now" reflects the idea that the incredible advancements in technology and innovation are shaping our lives and the world we live in today. Embracing these changes, addressing their challenges, and harnessing their potential for positive impact are key aspects of navigating the future. It underscores the importance of staying informed, adaptable, and forward-thinking in an ever-evolving world.

CONCLUSION

Remember that trading is not a guaranteed path to riches, but a disciplined and well-informed approach can significantly increase your chances of success. Here are some parting thoughts to carry with you on your trading journey:

1. **Education is Key:** Continuous learning is the cornerstone of successful trading. The financial markets are ever-evolving, and staying informed about new developments and strategies is essential.

2. **Risk Management is Paramount:** Protecting your capital should always be your top priority. Employ risk management techniques, set stop-loss orders, and avoid over-leveraging to safeguard your investments.

3. **Trading Psychology Matters:** Understanding your emotions and biases is crucial. Fear and greed can cloud judgment, leading to impulsive decisions. Developing discipline and emotional control is vital.

4. **Practice with a Demo Account:** Before risking real capital, practice your trading strategies on a demo account. This allows you to refine your approach without financial risk.

5. **Diversify Your Portfolio:** Avoid putting all your capital into a single asset or strategy. Diversification can help spread risk and enhance your chances of overall success.

6. **Keep Records:** Maintaining a trading journal is invaluable. It allows you to analyze your trades, identify patterns, and learn from your successes and mistakes.

7. **Seek Mentorship:** Learning from experienced traders or seeking professional guidance can accelerate your learning curve and help you avoid common pitfalls.

As you embark on your trading journey, remember that it's not just about making money but also about personal growth, discipline, and adaptability. The markets will challenge you, but they also offer boundless opportunities for those who approach them with diligence and a commitment to continuous improvement.

Trading is a lifelong pursuit, and each trade is an opportunity to learn, adapt, and refine your skills. As you navigate the exhilarating world of trading, may your journey be marked by success, resilience, and the fulfillment of your financial goals.

With this book as your foundation, you are now equipped to take your first steps into the world of trading, armed with knowledge, determination, and a mindset geared for success. Happy trading!

ABOUT THE AUTHOR

Arsene Junior Joseph, the author of "There is Hope," "Let's Try Jesus," "The Power of Imagination," "I Was Born for Greatness", "Truck Dispatching Master" "Devenez un Truck Dispatcher", "Retour A l'Agriculture en Haiti", "Mastering ChatGPT", "Wake Up" and "Increase Your Faith" is a multifaceted visionary with a remarkable journey encompassing diverse fields and a profound commitment to personal growth and community development. Hailing from the vibrant state of Florida, Arsene's life story is an inspiring testament to the pursuit of knowledge, creativity, entrepreneurship, and philanthropy.

A Lifelong Love for Learning

Arsene's journey into the world of knowledge commenced early in life. His profound love for reading led him to immerse himself in books, nurturing a voracious appetite for learning. This passion for the written word eventually evolved into a talent for crafting literary works, establishing him as an accomplished book writer and songwriter.

A Voice of Motivation and Inspiration

Arsene's gift for inspiring others is a central facet of his identity. He has embraced the role of a motivational speaker, sharing potent insights and empowering messages that guide individuals toward realizing their fullest potential. His speaking engagements have taken him across national and international boundaries, allowing him to connect with diverse audiences and disseminate his message of hope and personal development.

A Multifaceted Career

Arsene's professional journey is a reflection of his versatility and unwavering determination. He is not only a celebrated author and songwriter but also a thriving business owner. His entrepreneurial spirit has led him to explore various ventures, including MLM marketing, where he has achieved success through diligence and innovation.

In addition to his entrepreneurial pursuits, Arsene is a dedicated English teacher, imparting language skills and knowledge to others. His linguistic prowess extends beyond English; he is fluent in Spanish and French, enabling effective global communication and skilled translation services.

The Heart of a Philanthropist

Arsene's deep-rooted Christian faith has instilled in him a profound sense of philanthropy. He is committed to giving back to the community and actively supports charitable causes that align with his values.

A Handyman with a Heart

Beyond his intellectual pursuits, Arsene is a practical individual with a knack for problem-solving and assisting others. He has earned a reputation as a skilled handyman, always ready to lend a helping hand.

A Champion of Community Development

Arsene is not only passionate about personal growth but also community development. His dedication to this cause is evident through his involvement in various initiatives and organizations. He holds certificates in an array of fields, including fundraising concepts, business expansion, management strategies, community organizing, grant writing, and public-private partnerships, among others. His commitment to responsible leadership, transparency, and good governance reflects his belief in creating positive change at both local and global levels.

A Creative Soul

Arsene's creativity knows no bounds. In 2009, he had the privilege of collaborating with a renowned artist to write "Stop Boasting," a musical composition that resonated with audiences worldwide.

A Member of YLAI

Arsene is a proud member of YLAI (Young Leaders of the Americas Initiative), a prestigious program that empowers young entrepreneurs and change-makers to foster economic development and strengthen ties between the Americas.

Arsene Junior Joseph's life journey serves as a powerful example of the potential within each of us to lead a purpose-driven life. His dedication to learning, creativity, entrepreneurship, and community development embodies the spirit of a true visionary, inspiring others to follow their paths of growth and positive impact.

Arsene's deep and abiding love for Jesus Christ is a powerful testament to the transformative power of faith. His journey of devotion and unwavering commitment to Christ serves as an inspiration to many, reminding us of the profound impact that a personal relationship with Jesus can have on one's life.

Arsene's love for Jesus is not merely a superficial sentiment but a profound and life-altering experience. It's a love that has shaped his character, guided his decisions, and infused every aspect of his life with purpose and meaning.

WELL-KNOWN AND INFLUENTIAL TRADERS IN FOREX

1. **George Soros:** Known for "breaking the Bank of England" in 1992 by shorting the British pound. Soros is one of the most famous Forex traders in history.

2. **Paul Tudor Jones II:** A highly successful hedge fund manager and macro trader, known for his macroeconomic trading strategies.

3. **Stanley Druckenmiller:** Renowned for his partnership with George Soros and his successful Forex trading career.

4. **John R. Taylor Jr.:** Founder of FX Concepts, a leading currency hedge fund, and a respected figure in the Forex industry.

5. **Bill Lipschutz:** Lipschutz was a currency trader at Salomon Brothers and is known for his insights into Forex trading.

6. **Andrew Krieger:** Known for his aggressive trading style and his short-selling of the New Zealand dollar, Krieger gained recognition for his Forex trades.

7. **Bruce Kovner:** Founder of Caxton Associates, Kovner has had a successful career as a hedge fund manager, including Forex trading.

8. **Joe Lewis:** A British businessman and currency trader who has made significant investments in the Forex market.

9. **John Henry:** Founder of John W. Henry & Company, Henry has been successful in trading commodities and Forex.

10. **Richard Dennis:** Known for his involvement in the "Turtle Traders" experiment, which aimed to prove that trading success could be taught.

Please note that the Forex market is vast, and success can be found across various trading strategies and styles. These traders have made their mark in the industry through their unique approaches and significant achievements.

GLOSSARY OF KEY TERMS AND CONCEPTS

1. **Asset:** Anything with monetary value that can be bought or sold, such as stocks, currencies, commodities, or bonds.

2. **Bull Market:** A market characterized by rising prices and optimism among investors.

3. **Bear Market:** A market characterized by falling prices and pessimism among investors.

4. **Bid:** The highest price a buyer is willing to pay for a security.

5. **Ask (or Offer):** The lowest price a seller is willing to accept for a security.

6. **Broker:** An intermediary who facilitates the buying and selling of financial assets on behalf of clients.

7. **Leverage:** The use of borrowed capital to increase the potential return on an investment. It amplifies both gains and losses.

8. **Margin:** The amount of money or collateral required by a broker from a trader to open and maintain a position.

9. **Stop-Loss Order:** An order placed by a trader to automatically sell a security when it reaches a predetermined price, limiting potential losses.

10. **Take-Profit Order:** An order placed by a trader to automatically sell a security when it reaches a predetermined profit level.

11. **Volatility:** The degree of variation in the price of a financial asset over time, often used as a measure of risk.

12. **Market Order:** An order to buy or sell a security at the current market price, executed immediately.

13. **Limit Order:** An order to buy or sell a security at a specified price or better, but not at a worse price.

14. **Day Trading:** A trading style in which positions are opened and closed within the same trading day, with no overnight positions.

15. **Swing Trading:** A trading style that aims to capture shorter- to medium-term price swings or trends.

16. **Position Trading:** A long-term trading style where traders hold positions for an extended period, often weeks, months, or even years.

17. **Scalping:** A high-frequency trading style focused on making small, quick profits from very short-term price movements.

18. **Technical Analysis:** The analysis of historical price charts and patterns to predict future price movements.

19. **Fundamental Analysis:** The analysis of an asset's intrinsic value based on economic, financial, and qualitative factors.

20. **Diversification:** Spreading investments across different assets or asset classes to reduce risk.

21. **Margin Call:** A demand from a broker for additional funds to cover losses when a trader's account balance falls below a certain level.

22. **Liquidity:** The ease with which an asset can be bought or sold without significantly affecting its price.

23. **Hedging:** A strategy used to reduce or offset the risk of adverse price movements in one asset by taking an opposite position in another asset.

24. **Volatility Index (VIX):** A measure of market volatility often referred to as the "fear gauge."

25. **Pip:** The smallest price movement in the exchange rate of a currency pair in Forex trading.

26. **Candlestick:** A graphical representation of price movements on a chart, commonly used in technical analysis.

27. **Resistance:** A price level at which an asset tends to encounter selling pressure and struggles to move higher.

28. **Support:** A price level at which an asset tends to encounter buying interest and resists moving lower.

29. **Trend:** The general direction in which the price of an asset is moving over time, often categorized as bullish (upward), bearish (downward), or sideways.

30. **Risk-Reward Ratio:** The ratio of potential profit to potential loss in a trade, used to assess the trade's attractiveness.

31. **MACD (Moving Average Convergence Divergence):** A popular technical indicator used to identify changes in the strength, direction, momentum, and duration of a trend.

32. **RSI (Relative Strength Index):** A momentum oscillator used to measure the speed and change of price movements, indicating overbought or oversold conditions.

33. **Drawdown:** The peak-to-trough decline in the value of a trading account or investment portfolio.

34. **Arbitrage:** The simultaneous purchase and sale of an asset in different markets to profit from price discrepancies.

35. **Market Maker:** A financial institution or individual that provides liquidity by buying and selling assets, often in large quantities.

36. **Pip:** A unit of measurement for the change in value between two currencies in a currency pair, typically the fourth decimal place in most currency pairs.

37. **Rollover (Swap):** The interest paid or earned for holding a position overnight in the Forex market.

38. **Slippage:** The difference between the expected price of a trade and the actual price at which it is executed, often due to market volatility.

39. **Volatile Market:** A market characterized by rapid price movements and increased uncertainty.

40. **Quantitative Easing (QE):** A monetary policy tool used by central banks to stimulate the economy by purchasing financial assets, increasing the money supply.

Please note that this glossary provides an overview of key trading terms, but trading involves a wide range of concepts and strategies that go beyond these definitions. Traders should have a comprehensive understanding of these terms and consider seeking further education and professional advice when engaging in trading activities.

VARIOUS TRADING MARKETS AND EXCHANGES

1. New York Stock Exchange (NYSE)

2. Nasdaq Stock Market

3. London Stock Exchange (LSE)

4. Tokyo Stock Exchange (TSE)

5. Shanghai Stock Exchange (SSE)

6. Hong Kong Stock Exchange (HKEX)

7. Euronext

8. Frankfurt Stock Exchange (Frankfurter Wertpapierbörse)

9. Toronto Stock Exchange (TSX)

10. Australian Securities Exchange (ASX)

11. Bombay Stock Exchange (BSE)

12. National Stock Exchange of India (NSE)

13. Borsa Italiana (Italian Stock Exchange)

14. Swiss Exchange (SIX Swiss Exchange)

15. Madrid Stock Exchange (Bolsa de Madrid)

16. São Paulo Stock Exchange (B3)

17. Mexico Stock Exchange (Bolsa Mexicana de Valores)

18. Johannesburg Stock Exchange (JSE)

19. Moscow Exchange (MOEX)

20. Singapore Exchange (SGX)

21. Bursa Malaysia (Malaysian Stock Exchange)

22. Korea Exchange (KRX)

23. Taiwan Stock Exchange (TWSE)

24. Istanbul Stock Exchange (Borsa İstanbul)

25. Dubai Financial Market (DFM)

26. Abu Dhabi Securities Exchange (ADX)

27. Saudi Stock Exchange (Tadawul)

28. Qatar Stock Exchange (QSE)

29. Tel Aviv Stock Exchange (TASE)

30. Vienna Stock Exchange (Wiener Börse)

31. Oslo Stock Exchange (Oslo Børs)

32. Stockholm Stock Exchange (Nasdaq Stockholm)

33. Helsinki Stock Exchange (Nasdaq Helsinki)

34. Warsaw Stock Exchange (GPW)

35. Budapest Stock Exchange (Budapesti Értéktőzsde)

36. Prague Stock Exchange (Pražská burza)

37. Athens Stock Exchange (Athens Exchange)

38. Santiago Stock Exchange (Bolsa de Comercio de Santiago)

39. Buenos Aires Stock Exchange (Bolsa de Comercio de Buenos Aires)

40. Bogotá Stock Exchange (Bolsa de Valores de Colombia)

41. Lima Stock Exchange (Bolsa de Valores de Lima)

42. Caracas Stock Exchange (Bolsa de Valores de Caracas)

43. Nairobi Securities Exchange (NSE)

44. Johannesburg Stock Exchange (JSE)

45. Nigeria Stock Exchange (NSE)

46. Egyptian Exchange (EGX)

47. Casablanca Stock Exchange (Bourse de Casablanca)

48. Istanbul Gold Exchange (Istanbul Altın Borsası)

49. Multi Commodity Exchange (MCX, India)

50. Intercontinental Exchange (ICE)

51. Chicago Mercantile Exchange (CME Group)

52. Chicago Board Options Exchange (CBOE)

53. Eurex

54. Hong Kong Futures Exchange (HKFE)

55. Singapore Mercantile Exchange (SMX)

56. Dubai Gold & Commodities Exchange (DGCX)

57. Moscow Exchange Derivatives Market (FORTS)

58. Borsa İstanbul Derivatives Market (VIOP)

59. Johannesburg Stock Exchange Derivatives Market (Safex)

60. Osaka Securities Exchange (OSE)

61. Bursa Malaysia Derivatives Berhad (BMD)

62. Taiwan Futures Exchange (TAIFEX)

63. Borsa Italiana Derivatives Market (IDEM)

64. Euronext Derivatives

65. Eurex Exchange

66. Korea Exchange Derivatives Market (KRX)

67. Euronext Brussels Derivatives

68. Euronext Amsterdam Derivatives

69. Euronext Paris Derivatives

70. Euronext Lisbon Derivatives

71. Euronext Dublin Derivatives

72. Euronext Milan Derivatives

73. Euronext Oslo Derivatives

74. Euronext Zurich Derivatives

75. Euronext Growth Market Derivatives

76. CBOE Options Exchange

77. CME Group Options Exchange

78. NYSE American Options

79. NYSE Arca Options

80. NYSE National Options

Please note that this list includes various stock exchanges, commodity exchanges, and derivatives exchanges from different countries. Each of these markets specializes in specific asset classes and trading instruments, catering to a wide range of financial products and investment opportunities.

FINANCIAL MARKETS AND EXCHANGES

1. New York Stock Exchange (NYSE)

2. Nasdaq Stock Market

3. London Stock Exchange (LSE)

4. Tokyo Stock Exchange (TSE)

5. Hong Kong Stock Exchange (HKEX)

6. Shanghai Stock Exchange (SSE)

7. Euronext

8. Toronto Stock Exchange (TSX)

9. Bombay Stock Exchange (BSE)

10. National Stock Exchange of India (NSE)

11. Australian Securities Exchange (ASX)

12. Frankfurt Stock Exchange (FWB)

13. Singapore Exchange (SGX)

14. Borsa Italiana

15. São Paulo Stock Exchange (B3)

16. Swiss Exchange (SIX)

17. Moscow Exchange (MOEX)

18. Johannesburg Stock Exchange (JSE)

19. Korea Exchange (KRX)

20. Taiwan Stock Exchange (TWSE)

21. Dubai Financial Market (DFM)

22. Abu Dhabi Securities Exchange (ADX)

23. Bursa Malaysia

24. Tel Aviv Stock Exchange (TASE)

25. Istanbul Stock Exchange (BIST)

26. Mexican Stock Exchange (BMV)

27. Santiago Stock Exchange (SSE)

28. Buenos Aires Stock Exchange (BCBA)

29. Bolsa de Valores de Colombia (BVC)

30. Oslo Stock Exchange (Oslo Børs)

31. Stockholm Stock Exchange (Nasdaq Stockholm)

32. Helsinki Stock Exchange (Nasdaq Helsinki)

33. Warsaw Stock Exchange (GPW)

34. Prague Stock Exchange (PSE)

35. Budapest Stock Exchange (BSE)

36. Vienna Stock Exchange (Wiener Börse)

37. Athens Stock Exchange (ATHEX)

38. Euronext Brussels

39. Euronext Amsterdam

40. Euronext Paris

41. Euronext Lisbon

42. Borsa Istanbul (BIST)

43. Tadawul (Saudi Stock Exchange)

44. Qatar Stock Exchange (QSE)

45. Kuwait Stock Exchange (Boursa Kuwait)

46. Egyptian Exchange (EGX)

47. Casablanca Stock Exchange (BVC)

48. Johannesburg Stock Exchange (JSE)

49. Nairobi Securities Exchange (NSE)

50. Nigerian Stock Exchange (NSE)

51. Ghana Stock Exchange (GSE)

52. Bucharest Stock Exchange (BVB)

53. Belgrade Stock Exchange (BELEX)

54. Zagreb Stock Exchange (ZSE)

55. Ljubljana Stock Exchange (LJSE)

56. Bulgarian Stock Exchange (BSE)

57. Bucharest Stock Exchange (BVB)

58. Warsaw Commodity Exchange (WSE)

59. Riga Stock Exchange (Nasdaq Riga)

60. Vilnius Stock Exchange (Nasdaq Vilnius)

61. Tallinn Stock Exchange (Nasdaq Tallinn)

62. Zagreb Stock Exchange (ZSE)

63. Athens Exchange (ATHEX)

64. Istanbul Gold Exchange (IGE)

65. Kazakhstan Stock Exchange (KASE)

66. Tehran Stock Exchange (TSE)

67. Amman Stock Exchange (ASE)

68. Palestine Exchange (PEX)

69. Bahrain Bourse

70. Muscat Securities Market (MSM)

71. Colombo Stock Exchange (CSE)

72. Dhaka Stock Exchange (DSE)

73. Nepal Stock Exchange (NEPSE)

74. Karachi Stock Exchange (PSX)

75. Vietnam Stock Exchange (HoSE and HNX)

76. Ho Chi Minh Stock Exchange (HoSE)

77. Hanoi Stock Exchange (HNX)

78. Singapore Mercantile Exchange (SMX)

79. Dubai Gold and Commodities Exchange (DGCX)

80. Intercontinental Exchange (ICE)

81. Chicago Board Options Exchange (CBOE)

82. Chicago Mercantile Exchange (CME)

83. Chicago Board of Trade (CBOT)

84. New York Mercantile Exchange (NYMEX)

85. Commodity Exchange, Inc. (COMEX)

86. London Metal Exchange (LME)

87. Intercontinental Exchange (ICE Futures Europe)

88. Eurex

89. Osaka Securities Exchange (OSE)

90. Singapore Mercantile Exchange (SGX-DT)

91. Taiwan Futures Exchange (TAIFEX)

92. Zhengzhou Commodity Exchange (CZCE)

93. Dalian Commodity Exchange (DCE)

94. Shanghai Futures Exchange (SHFE)

95. Multi Commodity Exchange (MCX)

96. National Commodity & Derivatives Exchange (NCDEX)

97. Dubai Mercantile Exchange (DME)

98. International Petroleum Exchange (IPE)

99. European Energy Exchange (EEX)

100. CME Group (formerly Chicago Mercantile Exchange and Chicago Board of Trade)

Please note that this list is not exhaustive, as there are numerous other regional and specialized financial markets and exchanges worldwide. Each of these markets may specialize in trading specific types of assets, including stocks, bonds, commodities, derivatives, and more.

VARIOUS FINANCIAL MARKETS FROM AROUND THE WORLD:

1. Stock Market

2. **Foreign Exchange Market (Forex)**

3. Commodity Market

4. Bond Market

5. Cryptocurrency Market

6. Derivatives Market

7. Options Market

8. Futures Market

9. Money Market

10. Interbank Market

11. Equity Market

12. Precious Metals Market

13. Agricultural Commodities Market

14. Energy Commodities Market

15. Debt Market

16. Fixed-Income Market

17. Equity Index Market

18. Real Estate Market

19. Foreign Exchange Options Market

20. Cryptocurrency Exchange Market

21. Swaps Market

22. Over-the-Counter (OTC) Market

23. Carbon Emissions Market

24. Forex Spot Market

25. Forex Forward Market

26. Forex Swap Market

27. Mortgage-Backed Securities Market

28. Municipal Bond Market

29. Corporate Bond Market

30. Treasury Bond Market

31. Emerging Markets

32. Credit Default Swap (CDS) Market

33. High-Yield Bond Market (Junk Bond Market)

34. Mortgage Market

35. Consumer Loan Market

36. Stock Index Futures Market

37. Currency Futures Market

38. Interest Rate Futures Market

39. Agricultural Futures Market

40. Metal Futures Market

41. Energy Futures Market

42. Foreign Exchange Futures Market

43. Freight Futures Market

44. Livestock Futures Market

45. Options on Futures Market

46. Real Estate Investment Trust (REIT) Market

47. Peer-to-Peer Lending Market

48. Venture Capital Market

49. Private Equity Market

50. Angel Investment Market

51. Crowdfunding Market

52. Art Market

53. Antique Market

54. Rare Collectibles Market

55. Wine Market

56. Stamp Market

57. Vintage Car Market

58. Auction Market

59. Fine Jewelry Market

60. Fine Watch Market

61. Intellectual Property Market

62. Film and Entertainment Market

63. Music Rights Market

64. Carbon Credit Market

65. Betting and Gaming Market

66. Agricultural Commodity Options Market

67. Currency Options Market

68. Interest Rate Options Market

69. Real Estate Options Market

70. Credit Options Market

71. Freight Options Market

72. Insurance Market

73. Health Insurance Market

74. Life Insurance Market

75. Property and Casualty Insurance Market

76. Reinsurance Market

77. Crop Insurance Market

78. Weather Derivatives Market

79. Catastrophe Bond Market

80. Antique and Art Options Market

Please note that this list covers a wide range of financial and alternative markets, each with its unique characteristics and purposes. Additionally, new markets and financial instruments may emerge over time, reflecting evolving economic and technological trends.

SUMMARY

"Trading for Beginners" is a comprehensive guide that introduces newcomers to the world of trading, equipping them with fundamental knowledge, strategies, and key concepts. The book covers a wide range of topics to help readers understand the intricacies of financial markets and embark on their trading journey with confidence.

The book begins with a historical overview of money, exploring the evolution from barter systems and gold standards to modern-day paper money and digital currencies. It delves into the significance of these developments in shaping trading practices.

The chapters that follow elucidate what trading is and how it functions, underscore the importance of market analysis and trading strategies, and provide insight into the essential tools required for trading, from internet access and hardware to software platforms and charting tools. The book distinguishes between trading and investment, emphasizing their divergent approaches and goals.

The subsequent chapters delve into the intricacies of specific trading topics, such as the Forex market, strategies for making money in trading, Forex terminology, brokers and their significance, scams, commissions, and various analysis methods in trading.

The book also explores technical analysis in depth, covering topics such as candlestick charts, trends, trendlines, support and resistance, volume, and various chart patterns. Readers gain proficiency in analyzing market data and patterns.

It discusses significant changes and advancements in the trading world, from technology to regulations and strategies. Additionally, the book introduces fundamental analysis, emphasizing the role of economic calendars in trading decisions and how economic events can impact asset prices.

Risk management techniques are explained in detail, including position sizing, stop-loss orders, and diversification. The importance of stop-losses in limiting losses and protecting investments is emphasized.

The book provides insights into trading platforms, including popular tools like MetaTrader 4 (MT4) and TradingView, and covers essential aspects of trading success, from money management and trade analysis to protecting accounts and recording historical trades.

In conclusion, "Trading for Beginners" equips readers with a strong foundation in trading, making it a valuable resource for those entering the world of financial markets. Whether aspiring to become a full-time trader or seeking to diversify an investment portfolio, readers gain essential knowledge and skills to navigate the complex and dynamic trading landscape successfully. Happy trading!

POSITIVE QUOTES

1. "Success in trading starts with a mindset of discipline and patience."
   - Unknown

2. "The key to trading success is continuous learning and adaptability."
   - Jesse Livermore

3. "Every trade is an opportunity to learn and improve." - George Soros

4. "In trading, your losses are your best teachers." - Alexander Elder

5. "Risk comes from not knowing what you're doing." - Warren Buffett

6. "Trading is not about how much you make but how much you don't lose." - Bernard Baruch

7. "The markets are the sum of human psychology, and understanding them is the key to success." - Robert Kiyosaki

8. "Trading is not a game of chance; it's a game of skill and strategy." - Martin Schwartz

9. "Success in trading is about managing risk, not avoiding it." - George Soros

10. "The goal of a successful trader is to make the best trades, not necessarily the most trades." - Jack Schwager

11. "Trading is not about predicting the future; it's about managing the present." - Howard Marks

12. "The best investment you can make is in yourself, through education and self-improvement." - Warren Buffett

13. "The most important quality for a trader is emotional discipline." - Paul Tudor Jones

14. "Trading is not a sprint; it's a marathon. Stay focused on the long-term journey." - Unknown

15. "Trading is a journey of self-discovery. Know yourself, and you'll know the markets." - Jesse Livermore

16. "A successful trader is not the one who never fails but the one who never gives up." - Alexander Elder

17. "Trading is a puzzle, and every piece you solve brings you closer to success." - Martin Schwartz

18. "Don't let fear and greed drive your trading decisions. Stay disciplined and rational." - Warren Buffett

19. "Trading is not about being right all the time; it's about managing risk effectively." - Paul Tudor Jones

20. "Believe in your abilities, stay persistent, and success in trading will be yours." - Unknown

LIST OF SOME POPULAR CANDLESTICK PATTERNS AND CHART PATTERNS USED IN TECHNICAL ANALYSIS

Candlestick Patterns:

1. Doji

2. Hammer

3. Shooting Star

4. Bullish Engulfing

5. Bearish Engulfing

6. Morning Star

7. Evening Star

8. Harami

9. Dark Cloud Cover

10. Piercing Pattern

11. Hanging Man

12. Inverted Hammer

13. Three White Soldiers

14. Three Black Crows

15. Gravestone Doji

16. Dragonfly Doji

17. Marubozu

18. Spinning Top

19. Tweezer Tops

Chart Patterns:

10. Flag Pattern

11. Pennant Pattern

12. Symmetrical Triangle

13. Ascending Triangle

14. Descending Triangle

15. Wedge Pattern

16. Rising Wedge

17. Falling Wedge

18. Bullish Pennant

19. Bearish Pennant

20. Diamond Top

21. Diamond Bottom

22. Broadening Top

23. Broadening Bottom

24. Rounding Top

25. Rounding Bottom

26. Gaps (Common, Breakaway, Continuation, Exhaustion)

27. Island Reversal

28. Three Drives Pattern

29. Bearish Three Line Strike

30. Bullish Three Line Strike

LIST OF VARIOUS CANDLESTICK PATTERNS COMMONLY USED IN TECHNICAL ANALYSIS

Single Candlestick Patterns:

1. Doji

2. Dragonfly Doji

3. Gravestone Doji

4. Long-Legged Doji

5. Hammer

6. Hanging Man

7. Shooting Star

8. Spinning Top

9. Marubozu

10. Inverted Hammer

11. Rickshaw Man

12. Pin Bar

Two-Candlestick Patterns:

13. Bullish Engulfing Pattern

14. Bearish Engulfing Pattern

15. Bullish Harami

16. Bearish Harami

17. Piercing Line

18. Dark Cloud Cover

19. Morning Star

20. Evening Star

Three-Candlestick Patterns:

21. Bullish Three White Soldiers

22. Bearish Three Black Crows

23. Bullish Abandoned Baby

24. Bearish Abandoned Baby

25. Morning Doji Star

26. Evening Doji Star

27. Bullish Harami Cross

28. Bearish Harami Cross

29. Bullish Three Inside Up

30. Bearish Three Inside Down

Reversal Patterns:

31. Bullish Tweezer Bottoms

32. Bearish Tweezer Tops

33. Bullish Belt Hold Line

34. Bearish Belt Hold Line

35. Bullish Separating Lines

36. Bearish Separating Lines

37. Bullish Hikkake

38. Bearish Hikkake

39. Bullish Kicking

40. Bearish Kicking

Continuation Patterns:

41. Bullish Rising Three Methods

42. Bearish Falling Three Methods

43. Bullish Side-by-Side White Lines

44. Bearish Side-by-Side Black Lines

45. Bullish Upside Tasuki Gap

46. Bearish Downside Tasuki Gap

47. Bullish Counterattack Lines

48. Bearish Counterattack Lines

49. Bullish Unique Three River Bottom

50. Bearish Unique Three Mountain Top

These candlestick patterns are essential tools for traders and technical analysts to help them interpret price movements and identify potential trend reversals or continuations in the financial markets. Each pattern has its own significance and interpretation, and traders often use them in combination with other technical indicators to make informed trading decisions.

www.ingramcontent.com/pod-product-compliance
Lightning Source LLC
Chambersburg PA
CBHW072355290526
45794CB00001B/79